HARVEST OF HOPE

Stories of Life-Changing Gifts

KAY MARSHALL STROM

IVP Books

An imprint of InterVarsity Press
Downers Grove, Illinois

InterVarsity Press
P.O. Box 1400, Downers Grove, IL 60515-1426
World Wide Web: www.ivpress.com
E-mail: email@ivpress.com

InterVarsity Press® is the book-publishing division of InterVarsity Christian Fellowship/USA®, a student movement active on campus at hundreds of universities, colleges and schools of nursing in the United States of America, and a member movement of the International Fellowship of Evangelical Students. For information about local and regional activities, write Public Relations Dept., InterVarsity Christian Fellowship/USA, 6400 Schroeder Rd., P.O. Box 7895, Madison, WI 53707-7895, or visit the IVCF website at <www.intervarsity.org>.

Published in association with the Books & Such Literary Agency, Janet Kobobel Grant, 52 Mission Circle, Suite 122, PMB 170, Santa Rosa, CA 95409-5370, <www.booksandsuch.biz>.

All photographs are used by permission.

Design: Cindy Kiple
Images: boy pulling goats: David Sacks/Getty Images
        ribbon: Malcolm Romain/Istockphoto.com

ISBN 978-0-8308-3442-6

Printed in the United States of America ∞

Library of Congress Cataloging-in-Publication Data

Strom, Kay Marshall, 1943-
  Harvest of hope: stories of life-changing gifts/Kay Marshall
  Strom
      p. cm.
  ISBN 978-0-8308-3442-6 (pbk.: alk. paper)
  1. Church work with the poor. 2. Church charities. 3. Disaster
  relief. I. Title.
  BV639.P6S77 2007
  261.8'32—dc22
                                              2007011608

| P | 19 | 18 | 17 | 16 | 15 | 14 | 13 | 12 | 11 | 10 | 9 | 8 | 7 | 6 | 5 | 4 | 3 | 2 | 1 |
| Y | 23 | 22 | 21 | 20 | 19 | 18 | 17 | 16 | 15 | 14 | 13 | 12 | 11 | 10 | 09 | 08 | 07 |

CONTENTS

Acknowledgments

This book would not have been possible without open access to people around the world who have received donations through charitable catalogs. Because Partners International's *Harvest of Hope* is the catalog I knew best, I approached president/CEO Jon Lewis with a bold proposal: I wanted to travel the world and personally follow up on their projects. Uncensored, I said. Let me see firsthand what worked and what didn't work. He and his board agreed. And with surprising candor, Partners International opened their files to me. Thank you.

I especially thank Steven Downey, who assisted in this project, answering my endless questions and always making himself available to me. My thanks also goes to Tom Chandler, Mark Bardwell, Lisa Jonas and Kathie Delph who, from Singapore to Spokane, were quick to respond to my every query.

From the beginning, IVP editor Cindy Bunch listened to my idea and shared my enthusiasm. Thank you, Cindy.

People from many other ministries also made valuable contributions. They cheerfully cleared their busy calendars to make time to talk and to share their projects and approaches with me. I especially appreciate representatives from Samaritan's Purse, World Vision, World Relief and Direct Relief for making themselves so accessible. Special thanks to Amaro and Giselle Rodriquez, Jose and France-Lise Olivera, Dr. and Mrs. B. E.

Vijayam, Professor P. T. George and Rene Mbongo.

Many loving thank-yous to my husband, Dan Kline, who trekked through India, Cambodia, China and Indonesia with me, recording our travels on camera and camcorder, and thinking of questions that didn't occur to me.

Thanks to everyone around the world who opened their homes and lives to me. It is impossible to adequately express my gratitude for those amazing people who so encouraged and taught me by their examples of grace and courage in spite of circumstances.

And I extend a special thank you to every donor who has ever given through a catalog program. Although you may never have the privilege of meeting the one who received your gift, a special bond will always tie the two of you together. Please know that your gift to that one person is helping to change the world.

Thank you, all.

INTRODUCTION

Refugees, poverty, hunger and disease.

Floods, hurricanes, earthquakes and wars.

Every year brings its share of needs. Most usher in catastrophes as well. Sometimes disasters hit in such waves of devastation that the world can't get a moment to catch its breath. In 2005, for instance, while Southeast Asia was still reeling from the tsunami that killed almost a quarter of a million people, Hurricane Katrina plowed a huge swath through southern Mississippi and Louisiana, wiping out the city of New Orleans. Right on Katrina's heels, an earthquake in Pakistan's Kashmir region crushed forty thousand people and left many thousands more hungry and homeless to face a freezing winter. All that took place against a backdrop of atrocities in Sudan, war in Iraq, advancing HIV/AIDS infections and . . . well, you get the picture.

In such years, the media pour forth emotional pleas for help, and our mailboxes overflow. We are asked to donate and donate again and again and again.

People listen to the pleas. And they respond. In that one catastrophic year alone, Americans opened their wallets and gave close to five billion dollars for disaster relief. And, according to the Giving USA Foundation, as usual the bulk of charitable donations came not from the wealthy, but from individuals who chipped in their fifty or hundred or two hundred dollars. Folks like you and me.

**"I'd like to support a lesser-known project.
I think the big charities already get a lot of coverage."**

RACHEL M.

What happens when calamities strike, one on top of the other, when the urgency of disaster threatens to drown out the cry of everyday drought, starvation, poverty and disease? Donor fatigue. At least that's what some frustrated fundraisers tell us. So do newspaper and television reporters who periodically report on the plight of charities forced to cut their services and lay off workers because people have reached their emotional limit.

**"They say the Lord loves a cheerful giver,
but this giver's becoming less cheerful."**

**EIGHTY-SEVEN-YEAR-OLD WOMAN TO A REPORTER FROM THE
RICHMOND TIMES-DISPATCH ABOUT RECEIVING
260 REQUESTS FOR HOLIDAY CONTRIBUTIONS**

Others insist it isn't donor fatigue at all. People simply run out of money. Pockets are only so deep.

There is another possibility, of course. Perhaps the real problem is donor disappointment. These days, fewer and fewer of us are willing to simply write out a check and hand it over. Regardless of the emotional appeal, more of us look suspiciously at any place asking for our dollars and inquire, "Just exactly how much of my money would actually reach the people in need?"

Not a bad question.

After Hurricane Katrina, it was estimated that fully two-thirds of all Americans contributed to the relief effort. Within the first weeks alone, over half a billion dollars poured in to charities aiding victims of the flood. That's the good news. The bad news is that Americans' confidence that their money was actually making a difference plunged to less than

25 percent. People tossed in their money, all right, but they rarely saw evidence that it was helping in any tangible way.

> **"I like to be generous, but I want to know
> for sure where my money is going.
> I want to know it's really helping someone."**
> **BONNIE S.**

So how much trust do Americans place in charities as a whole? A recent New York University study found the following:

- A scant 11 percent said organizations do a very good job of spending money wisely.
- Two-thirds said charitable organizations waste a great deal or a fair amount of money.
- Almost half said leaders of charitable organizations are paid too much.

This is not surprising, what with all the charity scandals and scams making headlines these days. No one wants his or her hard-earned money to be misused. Even more, no one wants to feel taken in by grabby fundraisers.

> **"I seldom give, because I have too many questions."**
> **BEVERLY W.**

In Cambodia, I encountered a man who works for a U.S. government agency. When I commented that I would dearly love to discover that 90 percent of the money donated actually went to the needy, he snorted and said, "Ninety percent go to the people? Hah! More like 90 percent is wasted. The people are lucky to get 10 percent!" Not a statistic, to be sure, but an uncomfortable sign of widespread disillusionment, even among those deep in the trenches.

A common response to pleas for charitable giving is, "But the needs are overwhelming, and I can't do everything!" Of course not. No one can. Not even Bill and Melinda Gates, with all their resources.

And yet . . .

JESUS' TAKE ON THE POOR

Jesus commanded us to be compassionate and merciful and to help those in need. Throughout his ministry, he had much to say about the poor and what our response toward them should be. He went so far as to state that when you feed, clothe or minister to "one of the least of these brothers of mine," you do it for him (Matthew 25:37-40).

Sounds as though relief and care for the poor should be near the top of a Christian's agenda, doesn't it?

> **"Charity—giving to the poor—is an essential part of Christian morality. . . . If our charities do not at all pinch or hamper us, I should say they are too small."**
>
> **C. S. LEWIS**

When Hurricane Katrina hit New Orleans, people suffered terribly—even in the United States, with all the resources, agencies and infrastructure of the richest nation in the world. A year later, little progress had been made toward rebuilding the area. Just imagine, then, the effect disasters have on countries with no means to evacuate survivors or resettle people and no ability to meet their basic needs. Imagine what famine and war and poverty do in countries with absolutely no food or money to spare.

Yet simply feeling bad (or worse yet, guilty) about problems we didn't cause or situations we can't change won't make life better for anyone. Our charge is to act in constructive ways, to get involved in actively *doing good*. If we are to be effective in the face of worldwide misery, it's imperative that we think and act creatively.

"The first question which the priest and the Levite asked was:
'If I stop to help this man, what will happen to me?'
But . . . the good Samaritan reversed the question:
'If I do not stop to help this man, what will happen to him?'"
MARTIN LUTHER KING JR.

A NEW WAY

For over fifteen years, my sister Jo Jeanne crafted beautiful, handmade porcelain dolls. She had her own kiln for firing the heads and bodies. By the time she finished her painstaking work and put away her paintbrushes and sewing box, she had wonderful creations with silky hair and eyes that opened and closed, and they were dressed in handmade costumes. Everyone in the family received gifts of Jo Jeanne's lovely dolls. Before long, she started selling them at doll shows and through special orders.

Then Jo Jeanne began to show signs of multiple sclerosis. Inevitably the disease affected the fine motor skills she needed to make her dolls.

When I visited Jo Jeanne before Christmas one year, she told me wearily that she had just finished the last doll show she would ever do. Her kiln was up for sale. "I was afraid I wouldn't even make it through this Christmas season," she said. "I've been working nonstop for two months, and I'm absolutely exhausted." Then her face brightened as she added, "But I made more money than ever before!"

Now, that really stumped me. Jo Jeanne had never been driven by money. So in as circumspect a way as possible, I asked her, "What gives?"

"Subhas Sangma," she said.

Seeing my perplexed look, she said, "Come on, let me show you."

With a whole new wave of energy, my sister led me to her sewing room. There on the bulletin board, amid the patterns and fabric swatches, was a snapshot of a simple man in a white shirt. He was a pastor in Bangladesh, she explained, and for the past fifteen years, through a group called Partners International, she had donated all the proceeds from her doll business to his support.

> **"I can never go as a missionary.**
> **Someone else will have to be my hands and feet.**
> **I'll be the sender."**
> **JO JEANNE B.**

"But he and his wife are getting older, and they can't walk so many miles between villages in the beating sun and pouring rain," Jo Jeanne said. "They really need bicycles. My prayer was to earn enough money this Christmas to give Subhas Sangma one good last gift and then have enough left over to buy bicycles for him and his wife. And I did it!"

That was the first time I'd ever heard of Partners International. Or of the possibility of developing a long-term relationship with a person who spoke a different language and lived in a faraway country. Or of the idea of one ordinary person actually effecting a change in the life of someone she most likely would never meet.

> **"Every Christmas Day we sit down and 'spend' some money in**
> **Partners International's gift catalog. Just last week Mom said,**
> **'I wonder what happened to the family we got the goat for last year?'"**
> **CAROLINE P.**

A NEW WAY OF GIVING

It was several years later that I was given my first Partners International charitable gift catalog. In fact, it was the first time I'd ever *seen* such a catalog. I had great fun looking over the array of gift possibilities.

What a concept! Just plunk down twelve dollars, and in the name of my teacher friend, a child in China would get a chance at a future. Or for eleven dollars I could give the gift of fortified milk, and for the first time in his life a malnourished child in Sudan would go to bed without his tummy aching with hunger.

Or . . . yes, there it was. For $140, I could buy a bicycle for a pastor in Bangladesh.

> **"I believe that if you show people the problem
> and you show them the solutions they will be moved to act."**
> **BILL GATES**

I was hooked. Since the day I thumbed through that first catalog, I've collected gift catalogs from many organizations. The variety of gifts available is truly amazing. They run the gamut from cuddly toy lambs that play "Jesus Loves Me" (Samaritan's Purse, $4) to tuberculosis medicine for a patient in North Korea (Partners International, $7 per month) to two thousand fish to stock a village pond (World Concern, $20) to a library in a box (World Relief, $100) to twelve months of an Animal of the Month (World Vision, $3,690).

> **"I love doing this! I donated a dozen chickens from the
> Samaritan's Purse gift catalog in my dad's name last Christmas.
> He used to keep chickens."**
> **J. C. D.**

Maria Elena, whose son Ruben has Down syndrome, was overjoyed to find the perfect donor gift: sponsorship of a child with disabilities in North Africa. "I can't imagine what life would be like for Ruben without all the opportunities he has here," she said. "I want to do something to help a child get out of the back room and into a life of hope." Ahhh, right there is the strength of catalog donations: they allow people to tap into whatever it is that that touches their hearts.

**"For my birthday, my sister donated
a pig to a Chinese family and she named it Joe.
She wants to go to China and find Joe!"**

JOE K.

Not all donor catalogs are alike, of course. Some are specialized; others are more general. Some are faith-based; others are not. Some have unique sections, such as "Give Green," an earth-friendly part of Partners International Canada's catalog. Some include specific offerings for special events, such as Heifer International's "Joy to the World" selection, designed for company holiday parties, and its "Milk Menagerie," billed as a wonderful alternative appreciation gift for clients, customers and business associates, or World Concern's section "Corporate Opportunities."

**Erik, a student, received notification of a gift of a year's
education for a student in India given in his name.
Tobias, a landscape specialist, had rice seedlings donated
to a poor Cambodian family in his name.**

Catalogs can also help parents build giving hearts in even very young children. This was exactly the goal of John and Tauji when they involved their five-year-old son and two-year-old daughter in choosing their family's donations. "The problem was getting Eric to stop," Tauji said. "He wanted everything!" Although Eric was especially attracted to a boat (that looked like an awful lot of fun), they finally settled on animals for families in China and Cambodia, and they sponsored a street child in Senegal.

"It was a great beginning," Tauji said. "But next year we want to do a lot more. Not just at Christmas, but all through the year."

Some of the catalogs, such as those offered by Samaritan's Purse and Partners International, have a section specifically designed for kids. Donations can be made in children's names. Or, with their own money, children can donate something to which they personally relate—such as a soccer ball for a school in Iraq (eight dollars) or a flock of chicks to help a needy family get on its feet (ten dollars) or Bible story books for a Turkish Muslim child (six dollars).

> **"At first, our daughters didn't have much money.
> But even kids can put aside money
> and save it up for a project like this."**
>
> **PAT L.**

BUT DOES IT WORK?

That, of course, is the bottom-line question. Did the Chinese child given the gift of schooling in the teacher's name stay in school long enough to get an education? Is the Sudanese boy okay? And what about that pastor in Bangladesh? He may have a bicycle, but if no one gives him regular support, how can he continue to minister?

A long study conducted by ActionAid and Oxfam in the United Kingdom forecast that after all of the 2004 tsunami donation money was finally spent, only 20 percent would have directly delivered services to the victims. This was mainly because in the early days of that disaster, many aid agencies failed to coordinate and work together. In some villages, agencies competed to see who could hand out the most aid, while in others, starving people waited in vain for help that never arrived.

Does the same hold true with catalog giving? Do some people get flooded with flocks of chickens and baby goats while in other places children starve because no one donates for milk or food? Do organizations feel threatened by one another and refuse to work together? Just exactly what *is* the approach?

Good questions. Important ones. So before we go any further . . .

JUST WHAT MAKES FOR EFFECTIVE DEVELOPMENT AND RELIEF ANYWAY?

It's through lasting development that people grow in their ability to take control over their lives and improve the conditions that affect them. In the conclusion, we will discuss specific questions to ask when evaluating philanthropies, but are there basic concepts that make for effective development and relief projects? And do all organizations have to take the same approaches?

Yes, there are, and no, they don't. Consider child sponsorship. For a regular twenty-five or fifty dollars a month, a donor receives a child's picture and bio, sometimes notes from the child and, frequently, requests for extra gifts. But how exactly is that money used?

Well, it depends. For Compassion International, child sponsorship is the ministry. Its spokesman assured me that the child whose picture a sponsor receives is indeed the one who benefits from the donation. Oh, and each of Compassion's 3,500 children—all chosen on the basis of need—is connected to a church.

> **"Every Christmas my grandchildren get Heifer International gift cards in their Christmas stockings. Maybe it will inspire them for future Christmas giving."**
>
> **RON H.**

World Vision, however, has a different child sponsorship philosophy. Its overall goal is to enable communities and the people who live in them to reach their full potential by tackling the causes of poverty, and it sees child sponsors as critical to this end. So most of World Vision's sponsored children are just representatives of the needy kids living with their families in villages or communities. The child whose picture a donor receives doesn't exclusively benefit from the donation. Rather, that money is pooled with everyone else's money and used for projects benefiting all the community's children and families—a new school, say, or a well that provides clean water (although there are times when individual donations are used for a sponsored child's specific needs).

But what happens if a sponsor stops sending in donations? Does the child suddenly go from a full stomach to starving? from school back to the streets? Every child-sponsoring charity I interviewed responded with an emphatic "No way!" Children are always cared for until another sponsor is found. Still, as World Vision's representative emphasized, child sponsorship is not to be taken lightly. For when a sponsor drops out, "The child no longer benefits from a one-on-one relationship with a person who communicates with him and cares for him as an individual. Also, it affects the community."

> **"I know the little girl got milk and food she really needed, but I still don't understand how it was from me. How did I give it to her?"**
>
> **MADISON R., AGE 7**

An oft-expressed development concern is how to prevent *dependency in local communities.* "Actually, the key is preventing *unhealthy* dependency," Bob Savage, Partners International's director of international ministries, pointed out. "We look for local partners with their own vision. That vision doesn't change just because we provide money. Our partners already have their own track record. We simply come alongside and supplement it."

One way to prevent unhealthy dependency is to encourage "sweat equity" in a project, where local people make their own investment with their physical labor. Savage emphasized that this is something built into his organization's very foundation because "they are already working before we partner with them."

Gary Lundstrom, executive vice president of Samaritan's Purse, illustrated the same point by telling of a shipbuilding shop his organization set up after a group of fishermen lost their entire industry in a flood. Samaritan's Purse provided materials and a master shipbuilder, who gave guidance and oversaw the project, but the majority of the construction work on the forty boats was done by the fishermen themselves.

Another concept on which all the organizations agreed is the importance of Western groups and local people *making decisions together as partners*. World Vision's staff routinely meets and plans with community leaders for several months before they begin a long-term development program. "People with finance, knowledge and technology can provide advice and help, but they should not control the process," the organization's representative said. "People who are offered assistance play a vital part in defining what can be done and in implementing change. Participation is most effective when it empowers people to take control of their lives."

"Unity through humility," said Daniel Rickett, vice president of Sisters In Service (SIS).

> **"If you go to Africa, see if you can find the well our family bought for a village. Is it working?"**
>
> **DAN S.**

And what of the concept of *sustainability*? When the project is over, will the local people continue to reap its benefits? "We build sustainability into all the projects in our catalog," said Savage. "Almost every one builds people's capacity to better take care of themselves."

So does Heifer International, which works in fifty countries with the goal of providing animals—all the way from silkworms to elephants—to needy families so they can produce a salable product to support themselves. Heifer International requires that recipients pass the gift along by giving some of the animals' offspring to neighbors.

"Microenterprise development strengthens families."
GEORGE WASHINGTON UNIVERSITY STUDY

According to Rickett, that which people do for themselves and their communities tends to be not only most effective, but also most sustainable.

World Vision actively encourages self-sufficiency by helping communities access sustainable food sources, clean water and sanitation systems, homes, health care, education and income-generating skills. In 2006, nearly one million jobs were created or sustained worldwide as a result of its microloan programs.

Actually, microenterprise—offered in many of the catalogs—is an excellent example of built-in sustainability: A loan is given. With hard work and business counseling, a business develops, grows and produces income. The loan is repaid. The interest earned covers the cost of the lending program, and the repaid money is available for another business to take as a loan. According to World Vision, "Families flourish. Lives are changed. The circle is complete—and growing."

"Although clients are very poor, their repayment track records are remarkable. Money, mentoring and moxie make an outstanding mix."
WORLD VISION FIELD WORKER

Lundstrom offered this example: After a devastating disaster, Samaritan's Purse developed a training center in Indonesia where women were taught to sew. Then the organization helped them get sewing machines. The women set up their own independent businesses, and now they are completely self-supporting. Other women, who were taught to cook, opened a café. Today that café is successful and prosperous—and run solely by Acehnese people.

Yet for development projects to be truly effective, *local culture and community context must be considered*. These aren't just projects, after all.

They are drastic changes that affect the lives of real, living, feeling human beings.

"But everyone knows, those people would be better off if . . ." Really? *Everyone* knows?

Many a project has crashed and burned because an agency charged forward, completely convinced that the only relevant sensibilities were its own and those of its donors.

"For Partners International, local context is the whole point," said Savage. "Our programs are all directed from our local partners." A World Vision representative said, "More than 95 percent of our staff is indigenous to the nations where we work. Participation is most effective when it respects people's knowledge and skills."

Unfortunately, not all organizations adhere to this simple caveat. Lundstrom told of sitting under a sheltered structure rebuilt by another group after the 2004 tsunami destruction. "What is this place?" he asked. He was told it was the marketplace. "But the marketplace is always the busiest place in town," he said. "Why is no one here?" Because no one had bothered to consult the locals, and it had been built on the wrong side of the courtyard. Now the townspeople refused to use it. The group who built it simply snapped a few pictures for their donors and left.

This is exactly why Samaritan's Purse makes certain that when it takes its signature program, "Operation Christmas Child," into a new country, it knows the ground rules of the area. In places under Muslim control, for instance, its workers first ask local officials for permission, then they contact the local imams.

Despite all the planning, an organization must be willing to *adapt and learn from changing circumstances*. Partners International established a training center in Timbuktu, Mali, where women were taught to sew. The center was incredibly successful, with one hundred women completing the course each year. Trouble was, Timbuktu is an awfully small place for so many seamstresses. But since the program operators were right there locally, they quickly saw that many women could not find work in the saturated market. They responded by starting a bakery and teaching women to bake. Now the center has a second hugely successful enterprise, and it's ready to start a third.

While these guidelines will help form a foundation for considering the projects in the following chapters, the answer to healthy development is in the process, as Rickett pointed out. "Accompanying people in the business of life, making the journey with them and supporting those who can do this—that's the solution," he said. "Through faith in God, it's pointing people to justice, peace and hope."

THE REST OF THE STORY

Armed with the promises made in gift catalogs, I set out to follow up with the people who were in the best position to know the realities—those who had actually received donations. I wanted to find out the degree to which they and their villages truly were affected by those gifts of twenty-five, fifty and two hundred dollars you and I donate.

"You keep our hope alive. Hope keeps us going."
AMINA, SUDANESE REFUGEE

Partners International kindly opened their catalog projects to me, allowing me to observe their sites around the world and to interview freely—uncensored and without obligation. To observe not only the successes but also the stumbles and difficulties. The examples in the book were taken from the Partners International catalog (and are subject to change). However, many other organizations sent me catalogs, granted me interviews and graciously answered my questions.

Now I invite you: Come along with me and judge for yourself. We'll go to the refugee camps of Sudan, to North Africa and Senegal. We'll visit India, Cambodia and China. We'll spend time in Indonesia to see how true catastrophes are handled. Because this book is organized by subjects rather than by geography, we will sometimes visit several countries in one chapter. At other times we will return to a country we have previously visited and see a different program.

Along the way, you will meet some amazing people who find hope in the most challenging of circumstances.

We've seen the appeals. Now let's see "the rest of the story."

A NEW KIND OF BANKING

Kong Sey* looked worn away by life. Bony and toothless, he tugged his ragged T-shirt down over the sarong tied around his skinny waist. Yet when he motioned us to follow the clunk of a wooden cowbell to where his cow was munching grass, her four-month-old calf nestled up against her, Kong's weathered face broke into a proud grin.

"Does she have a name?" I asked.

"I call her Blessing," Kong answered. "She is my blessing cow."

One year earlier, Kong had been selected to receive the first cow from the animal bank his church had just organized. It was a real honor. Yet it also required an act of faith on his part. While he didn't have to pay anything for the cow, it would cost him plenty before he would realize a profit. Blessing didn't have a first calf for nine months, and that baby was owed to the animal bank to repay

> **COW FOR A FAMILY**
>
> With the average Cambodian family's income only three hundred dollars a year, most families cannot afford a dairy cow. Your gift will provide milk for malnourished children and increase the family income as they sell the dairy products. It will also allow them to start a family business. **$350**

---

*Because of the sensitivity of the areas covered in this book, all names, specific locations and identifying details have been changed.

Kong's "loan." Yet all that time, the cow had to be fed and cared for and kept healthy. Should she get sick, the expenses could pile up quickly. It would be close to another year before Blessing had a second calf. If Kong wanted to get the best possible price, he would have to wait until that baby was almost grown before he offered it for sale. No small commitment for a poor farmer in Cambodia, where the average annual income is just three hundred dollars.

Calling his son to help, Kong untied his cow and proudly led her over for us to admire. His son followed with the calf. In their community, simply to own such an animal marked Kong as a successful man.

He continued to plow his small plot of land by hand. In his opinion, Blessing was far too valuable to hook up to a plow. The cow was doing her part, he told us, by contributing fertilizer for his crops. Never before had he been able to afford such a luxury.

> **PIGLET FOR A POOR FAMILY**
>
> Many Cambodian villagers barely have enough money to buy basic food items, and they remain in poverty for generations. Your gift provides one piglet for a family to raise and helps bring them out of poverty and provide education for their children. **$25**

Anyway, he explained, "Her job is to have babies." Even though two of her calves would have to go to the cow bank to keep the program going—the third as well as the first—there would be many for him to sell. Kong expected Blessing to have twelve or thirteen calves during her lifetime. Maybe as many as fifteen. And each could bring him more money than he would otherwise earn in an entire year.

"But the most important thing is that she belongs to me," he said, his grin widening. "I finally have something that is really my own."

UNDERSTANDING CAMBODIA

Since the early 1990s, Cambodia has grabbed the attention of many do-

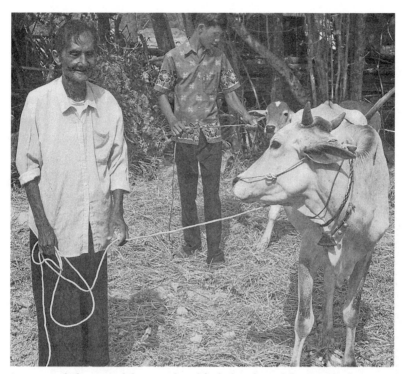

A cow named Blessing and the man whose life she has changed (by Dan Kline)

nors and donor groups around the world. World Vision, for instance, began working in health, agriculture and skills training for people disabled by land mines. It has also consistently been in the forefront of small-business development and microcredit programs.

Despite good intentions, other donations have missed the mark. We passed a small clinic in a village outside Phnom Penh that was built and paid for by good-hearted donors several years earlier. Totally outfitted and fully supplied, it stood abandoned and slowly falling apart. The clinic had never been used. What the donors hadn't realized is that there is not one doctor in the entire area.

Cambodia, a unique country where karma and fatalism reign, is mostly made up of Buddhists who believe in reincarnation. Cambodians tend to attribute everything that happens to destiny, ordained by actions in previous lives. They also believe they are likely to get caught up in punishment rained down on others who have committed evil deeds.

And few countries have known more evil than Cambodia. Between 1975 and 1979, Pol Pot and his Khmer Rouge turned the entire country into one murderous labor camp. They emptied cities and towns, ordering millions of people to the countryside, where they were forced to work as agricultural slaves in what became known as the "killing fields." Money was abolished, schools were closed, newspapers shut down, and all religion was banned.

When I asked Kong about those awful days, his grin faded and a shadow fell across his face. In a hushed voice, he spoke of his first family. "Pol Pot's people came and moved everyone away from here," he said. "My family and my neighbors . . . all of us. Our village was too close to the city, they said. So they moved us away from my birthplace to a very remote area."

Although Kong had been a farmer all his life, that was not the job assigned him. "My job was to catch fish. There was no salt, no gasoline, no anything in those days. We tried to catch a few extra fish so we could trade them for the things we needed. Fish was like money to us. It was the only money there was."

After fishing most of the day, Kong and his neighbors were sent to the mountains to cut wood to make into fish traps. Then, as the day was ending, they were ordered to the rice paddies to begin work there.

At least village people such as Kong knew how to work with their hands. City people knew nothing about growing rice or catching fish. Certainly not about doing physical labor from before dawn to far into the night with only the most rudimentary of tools. Countless people died of exhaustion, disease and starvation. "My wife died in the rice paddies," Kong said, his eyes filling with tears at the memory. "And all three of my children. They all died. In my whole family, only I remained alive."

The Khmer Rouge tortured and killed anyone they considered educated. This included not only professionals and business people, but anyone who spoke a second language. Or who wore glasses. Nearly two million Cambodians perished in those four years—almost a quarter of the country's population.

Pol Pot's horrific rule ended abruptly when Vietnam invaded Cambodia in 1979. Ten years later, the Vietnamese withdrew. Not until 1990 did Cambodia finally know a full year of peace. But by then, the country was in ruins. No doctors or teachers or builders or engineers were left alive. No craftsmen of any kind. A whole new generation had to learn everything from scratch. The church also had to start all over again. In 1990, only two thousand Christians lived in the entire country. They worshiped together in two hundred house churches. In all of Cambodia, only two Christian ministers were known to have survived.

Still today Cambodia is one of the world's poorest countries. It continues to suffer from a virtual absence of basic infrastructure. Professionals such as doctors and teachers are in short supply.

Yet in 2005, the Evangelical Fellowship of Cambodia estimated the number of evangelical Christians to be 200,000, and they identified 23,000 churches. That's an 11,400-percent increase in churches in just fifteen years! It has come about almost totally through the efforts of the indigenous Cambodian church.

ENTER ANIMAL BANKS

Most of Cambodia's churches are poor, led by people with no leadership training and conducted in a room in someone's house. Whoever has been a Christian the longest steps forward and takes charge. In this solidly Buddhist country, the church's method of growth has been quite simple: reach out to the community with the love of Christ.

In a country such as Cambodia, where almost everyone is poor, few people have access to bank loans. Even if they did, they would have no means of paying them back. And so people simply resigned themselves to poverty. That is, they did before the churches introduced the idea of animal banks.

"It's the people's first foray into the concept of banking," said David, the area's facilitator from Partners International. He had received his training through World Relief, under a mentor who had set up cow banks in Bolivia. That program helped extremely poor mothers with young children by enabling each one to get a calf to raise. Years later, David's mentor returned to Bolivia and was absolutely amazed by what he saw. Those once struggling mothers had become ranchers! Every one of them had a small herd of cows. No longer were they considered poor; now they were women of means. Their children were able to go to the university.

"I was excited about the idea for Cambodia," David said. "Poor house churches can conduct animal banks on their own."

In many areas of the world, World Vision is able to act as a bank for groups that need to borrow money for microfinance projects. These acting banks lend money, calculate interest and hold borrowers accountable. When I set out to visit the first of Cambodia's animal banks, I thought I would see a headquarters building. I pictured myself sitting down with members of the board, interviewing them and asking them questions. But I quickly discovered that animal banks are pretty much invisible. That is, unless you find a man like Kong Sey, then trace back to the church that sponsored him (Faith Church), and then back to the person in that church who actually advanced him the cow (Pastor Luke).

Although the banks are run by individual churches, this animal banking program is overseen by the Khmer Evangelical Association (KEA), a small organization of nineteen churches located in seven of Cambodia's twenty-four provinces. (This isn't the only organization doing this work. The River of Life, which also runs animal banks, is a much larger organization with 170 churches in sixteen provinces, mostly in extremely remote areas.)

Each church chooses its own development committee, which in turn decides who will benefit most from receiving a cow. This is where donors come in: when more people choose to donate animals, more animals are available to the banks to give to more people like Kong.

Churches receive a basic one-page lender contract that they can adjust and modify to fit their particular situations. At Faith Church, for instance, the question came up of who would be responsible should an animal die. Recipients are so poor, it would be catastrophic for them to have to pay for a lost cow. On the other hand, should the animal bank have to cover such losses, the entire system could collapse. It was a matter of compassion versus sustainability. Their solution was to place two veterinarians on their board. Under their guidance, the animal bank committee provided careful instructions to everyone who received an animal. "They taught me how to feed my cow and what problems to watch for," Kong said. "That's why she is so beautiful today."

According to the church's contract, if an animal dies through carelessness (skimping on food to save money, for instance, or neglecting its medical needs), the recipient has to pay. But if the animal dies through no fault of the owner, the recipient and the church each pay half the cost.

Right now the Cambodian church animal banks have no water buffalo or goats. They did have chickens, but they weren't profitable, so most were sold. At present they just have cows and pigs.

Pigs are an excellent short-term project. Min Panyaa got a sow that soon had a litter of eight piglets. Next time, Min is hoping for twelve babies. With such a yield, she can raise a lot of pigs quickly. Because she really needed the money, she repaid the animal bank and immediately sold the other piglets while they were still young. (A two-month-old piglet goes for forty dollars.) But even though it costs more to hold on to the piglets and raise them to adulthood, Min plans to keep the next litter until they are grown. "Then I can sell them for twice as much," she said.

Pigs provide a nice profit and a faster return on investment. Yet there is a downside to raising them: they have a lower survival rate than cows. Min's neighbor had an entire litter wiped out by disease. Then there's the high price of pig feed. When a poor family has only one pig, it can be fed slop and table scraps. But when they suddenly have ten hungry young pigs, they have to buy food for them. Sometimes struggling families will actually take food from their children to keep their pigs alive long enough to get them to market.

It costs about two hundred dollars to raise a litter of pigs, but if all goes well, a recipient can clear about two hundred dollars in profit. Not bad for a six-month investment.

Cows sell for around four hundred dollars, but it takes much longer to earn a profit from them. So, unlike Kong, many recipients set their cows to work plowing the fields to help pay their way.

KEA churches run twenty-two cow banks. Each starts with one cow and grows as participants repay with female calves. (The bank only wants females. If a calf is male, it must be raised to adulthood and then sold so that a female can be purchased and given to the bank.) Because the churches decided to require that two calves be repaid, the banks are growing much more quickly and are stronger. This allows the banks to help more people—although it is harder on the recipients.

"It's naive to think people are too poor to repay a loan," David said. "So far, everyone who has received an animal from these banks has repaid. This is what helps this program sustain itself."

Just as other churches in the animal bank program, Faith Church has no problem finding applicants for a pig or a cow. In fact, both programs have waiting lists.

Meeng Sophany, who got a cow last year, told how her daughter gets up early and goes out every morning to gather armloads of grass from surrounding fields to feed the cow and its calf. "Your cow is really beautiful," I told her as I petted its velvet-soft nose.

She smiled shyly. "I wash her every day."

I asked if it was a difficult decision to take on the cost and task of raising a cow. "No!" Meeng answered without hesitation. "I wanted the cow. I could always see the potential."

For her, that potential included an education for her daughter, as well as for her little boy, who hung back shyly in the shadows. Studying alongside her children, Meeng was just starting to learn to read and write. "It will be different for them," she said. "They won't have to wait and learn when they're grown. Because of the cow, life will be different for my children."

BECAUSE OF A COW

Kong Sey has been feeding Blessing for more than a year, and her calf for several months. "It's the dry season now, so I have to buy the food," he said. He keeps his cow close by, where he can hear the clatter of her wooden bell, for he must always be on the lookout for thieves. He still has at least another year before he will have a calf to sell.

So, does he consider Blessing worth all the work and investment? "Oh, yes," he exclaimed. "She is well worth it. And especially when I see the next baby. It will be mine."

"The animal banks strengthen the church by helping the poor," said Pastor Luke. "They give our people a way to help themselves."

KEY BENEFIT: This gift not only provides income for poverty-level families; it also gives the emerging church in Cambodia a unique opportunity to grow both in numbers and in strength as it administers the animal banks.

KEY CHALLENGE: The lack of trained leadership both to guide the programs and to form new churches as people come into the church as a result of the animal banks.

RICE SEEDLINGS FOR A FAMILY: *Cambodia*

So, who should receive this allotment of rice seedlings from the church's rice bank? Several names had been suggested to the committee, and now Pastor Luke, Pastor Ney and Elder Pok were charged with making the final decision.

"I cast my vote for Nhem Chea," said Pastor Luke.

The other two nodded their agreement. At sixty-eight, Nhem, a widow, was struggling to raise her four grandchildren alone. She was earning less than a dollar a day, and that was at a seasonal job.

"Nhem Chea, then?"

Yes, everyone agreed. She was the right choice.

RICE—THE CHURCH'S OTHER BANK

The banking program isn't limited to animals. In Cambodia, the churches also operate rice banks that enable poor church members to start raising their own rice crops. These banks are doing especially well. Just inside the front doors of Grace Evangelical church, Pastor Ney opened a side door onto a room piled floor to ceiling with bulging sacks. "All rice," he told us.

> **RICE SEEDLINGS FOR A FAMILY**
>
> There is an urgent need to provide rice seeds for desperately poor families who lost their crops due to flooding. Your gift allows church members and villagers to recover their crops and retain their primary source of income. **$60**

In this one church alone, the rice bank collected about twenty tons of rice. That was because people paid back their loans in rice from the harvest. And these rice repayments could be used to buy more seedlings, which could then be distributed to people such as Nhem.

But the rice bank benefits the church in another way as well. Although church members have no money, and in some cases have barely enough to feed their families, they faithfully tithe what they do have—their rice. At harvest time, they bring a portion to the church and present it as an offering to God. This donated rice is set aside to relieve hunger in the community. For eleven years, members of Grace Evangelical Church have been doing this—ever since the church was only a handful of people meeting together in a home.

Church members regularly go house to house to determine who in the village is in the most desperate need. Buddhist, atheist, Christian—religion makes no difference. The simple criteria are poverty and hunger. But when church members make their gifts, they let recipients know it's coming to them from the church in the name of Jesus.

This demonstration of selfless love has gone a long way toward drawing people into the church—people such as Kong, Min, Meeng and Nhem. As the community sees the church demonstrating Christ's love in action, they grow eager to learn more about the source of that love. As Kong said, "We go from no hope to hope because of Jesus."

From the original group of five people who gathered together to worship in a home, Grace Evangelical Church has grown into a congregation of about a hundred people who meet in their own church building. Ask Pastor Ney about this growth and he will say, "It's because of the rice bank."

"This rice will last for a short time only," Nhem said of the bag of rice she received along with her allotment of rice seedlings. "But God has changed my life, and that will last forever."

A TRUE SUCCESS STORY

"We have had very good profits in our rice bank," Pastor Luke told us, "and we used those profits to buy sewing machines for the church." This was an exciting move because it opened up a whole new area of potential. Church members can use the sewing machines for tailoring and altering clothes, as well as for making household items to sell. By allowing poor families to earn extra money, individual microenterprises bring them closer to the goal of individual self-sufficiency.

Yet the gains Cambodian church members have realized from their rice banks reach far beyond the financial. Investing in their future has empowered them. Many groups have come in, offering the people a handout—often dispensing it with a hefty dose of pity. But in the banking program, church members are treated as business people. Though no commercial bank would give them a second look, they can sign their name to an official agreement and, on the strength of their signature, receive help and hope for a future. Loans are granted with every expectation and confidence that recipients will fulfill the terms of the contract. Everyone simply assumes the money will be repaid. And the people have responded by doing exactly that. Every one of them.

"This is extremely important to poor people who are usually assumed to be unable to manage money," David said. "It's treating them with respect and dignity, and they're very responsive to it."

Furthermore, despite their own poverty, church members are given the opportunity to help others who are in even more desperate circumstances. "The gospel of the Lord Jesus Christ is being made known in the villages through the rice seedling project," said Pastor Luke. "Even the local government recognizes that Christian love is helping many people in need."

While the animal bank still needs donors—as does the rice bank— the rice bank appeal that appears at the beginning of this section will be removed from Partners International's gift catalog. Pastor Luke reports that the banks have had such an excellent repayment rate that they will no longer be asking for disaster assistance to protect them against times of flood and drought. They can now manage such emergencies on their own.

What a change for a people who have suffered so long and have lost so much. What a change of mindset for a population raised to accept fate with hopeless resignation. The animal and rice banks have given them an entirely new vision. "I tell them what they're doing is for the long term," said David, "for fifty years from now. Who knows what Cambodia will be like by then? I tell them to think about how they will be able to help other countries fifty years from now. If God continues to bless them, just imagine what their ministry might be like!"

KEY BENEFIT: This gift not only provides a road to self-sufficiency for impoverished families, it also gives the emerging church in Cambodia a unique opportunity to reach out to the community in Christ's name and to grow and strengthen in the process.

KEY CHALLENGE: The poverty of the churches, coupled with the lack of trained leadership.

2

SUFFER THE LITTLE CHILDREN

Looking out over the horizon, I could see nothing but tattered shelters spread over a sun-baked landscape of sand . . . and sand . . . and still more sand—hopelessness viewed through a yellow-brown cloud of blowing grit. Only nine o'clock in the morning, and already the sun scorched my skin right through my clothes.

I'd just left a crumbling room filled with young children singing, dancing and playing games. Dedicated teachers were doing their best to help the little ones recover from trauma I couldn't even imagine.

"People ask me, 'When is a good time to come to Khartoum?'" a willowy medical student had told me the day before. "I tell them the truth: 'There is no good time.'"

Yet people do come. Thousands upon thousands of them. Not because they want to, but because they have nowhere else to go. Fleeing war and starvation in places like the Congo and Uganda—and most of all, southern Sudan—people are literally running for their lives. All are displaced—men, women and children.

EDUCATION FOR A CHILD

Many children in southern Sudan have never attended school because most schools were destroyed during the civil war. You can send a child to a Christian primary school sponsored by Partners International, where education, supplies, a daily meal and hope for the future are provided. . . . **$9/month or $108/year**

A Sponsored Child

"Hello, Ruth," I said to the twig-thin eight-year-old who stood before me in the office. Solemn-faced and unblinking, she stared at me in silence.

I smiled. She didn't smile back. I offered her a chair. She stood. "Coca-Cola?" I suggested. She shook her head.

Ruth simply fixed her huge dark eyes on me and stared.

I already knew something of the little girl's story. Five years earlier, after a harrowing escape from southern Sudan, her just-widowed mother managed to make it to this refugee camp with Ruth and her baby sister in tow.

But Ruth has another family too—her sponsors. They live in Nebraska, and every month, along with money for her schooling, they send her candy and a letter with pictures of their family. And every month they assure her they pray for her every day.

"Tell me, Ruth," I said, "what's the best thing about living here in this camp?"

"School," she answered. "I can study and go to school here. But my mother says if we go back home, maybe I can't do that anymore." Her mother may be right. With most schools in the south destroyed after a quarter-century of civil war, an entire generation of children has never had a chance to attend school.

Schools are available in northern Sudan, however. Which would be good news, except for one troubling twist. Sudan's Muslim government requires that all children go through Koranic kindergarten before they can be accepted into primary schools. And, beginning with kindergarten, all school children are intentionally and systematically indoctrinated in Islam. Horrifying indeed to the majority of southern Sudanese who are Christian.

To protect children from this indoctrination, the African Inland Church of Sudan (AIC) now operates two Christian schools in the Khartoum area, which together accommodate more than three hundred children. These are vitally important, they say, because Christian education at an early age will help establish a strong foundation that will enable children to better stand up to the challenges of the Islamic educational system when they are older.

Problem is, many Christian families struggle simply to survive. In this Muslim-dominated area, finding a job is no easy task for a Christian. They simply cannot afford to send their children to a Christian school. To make matters worse, the government recently built a large elementary school near AIC's two Christian schools. The government offers free education, free uniforms and free food for the children. No cost for anything. But all is based on Islam.

"Most of these children have lost their fathers in the war," said Reverend James Lagos, an AIC leader in Khartoum. "Children often go to school without breakfast and also without dinner the night before. You can see in their faces that they are miserable with hunger. Mothers don't want to send their children to these Islamic schools, but with no money for tuition or even for food, what choice do they have?"

Well, they have us. Children such as Ruth, who is sponsored through Partners International's Sponsor A Child program, are able to attend AIC Christian schools. Not only are they provided with a good learning environment and school tuition, but they also get a nutritious meal every day. They receive textbooks and other school supplies—even clothes if they need them. And sponsors can be assured that the money they send to "their child" is spent on that child's schooling and personal needs.

At this writing, AIC operates eleven schools throughout Sudan: three preschools, seven primary schools and one secondary school. Their major goal is to reduce illiteracy and to educate the next generation. They are achieving this goal, and they are doing even more. They're equipping the future church of Sudan.

"What do you want to be when you grow up?" I asked Ruth.

"A doctor," she said. "I will study and study if I get a chance." This place could certainly use another doctor. How fortunate that a family in Nebraska is committed to giving Ruth that chance.

MUSLIM SCHOOL

Thomas lives in the same refugee camp as Ruth, but he doesn't go to the same school. Unlike Ruth, he doesn't have the benefit of a sponsor. At thirteen, Thomas is only in the fourth grade.

"He attends a Muslim school," his mother said. "With ten children in our house—counting our six orphaned nieces and nephews—and with my husband only getting part-time work, we can't afford to pay for school. We have no choice."

Thomas gets free food at the Muslim school, which his struggling mother appreciates. But the boy is also fed a constant diet of strict Islamic curriculum. That she doesn't like at all. "Every night I read the Bible to him before he goes to bed, then I read it again before he goes to school in the morning. But still my son comes home quoting the Qur'an," she says. "Well, why not? That's what he hears all day long. But what can I do? What can I do?"

A CHILD ALONE

Stranded in the depths of no work, with the pleading cries of orphaned family members calling out to them for help—that's where many desperate Sudanese families find themselves. They are, quite simply, pushed beyond endurance.

One mother told me about six-year-old Hajousif, a new arrival at the camp. His aunt and uncle were already stretched to the limit when a neighbor showed up at their door carrying the scrawny boy. He had found Hajousif wandering, hungry and alone. "I recognized him as your kin, so I brought him to you," the neighbor said. "It's up to you to take him in."

They did, grudgingly. They had no choice.

Hajousif's aunt and uncle kept him busy gathering firewood for the older children to sell. When the day's one meal was ready, Hajousif wasn't allowed to eat with the family. He sat quietly in the corner with his hands folded until everyone else finished. Then he got whatever was left—if anything was left. If not, he went to bed hungry.

Hajousif's uncle enrolled him in the Muslim kindergarten. But the school officials reported that, although they punished the boy every day, he would not eat with the other children. He would sit in the corner with his hands folded until they were finished. Only then would he creep over and eat their leftovers.

"And if Hajousif had a sponsor?" I asked. "What then?"

"I don't know," said the other mother. "His aunt and uncle are who they are."

AND THE FUTURE?

I asked Thomas, "If you could be anything in the world when you grow up, what would you be?"

"I'd be a pilot," he replied without hesitation.

"A pilot!" I responded in surprise. "Why is that?"

"So I could fly away from here," he said. "I want to go someplace where no one is killing everyone else."

I asked Ruth if she had one message she would like to give everyone in the world. "Yes," she said. "I'd like to tell them to love and not hate. Please, please . . . just don't hate each other."

As the children left, I stepped outside to wave goodbye. The sun, not yet at its zenith, roasted the barren ground. A thermometer tacked on the wall read a sizzling 118 degrees. Hot winds whipped up the sand and sent it whirling high into the air.

Heat and sand. War and hunger. Death and destruction.

What kind of a future could these children possibly have?

Unless . . .

"I thank God that Ruth is in a Christian school," her mother told me. "She has a chance to learn and study. Maybe she can make something good out of her life."

Thomas also had a message for the world: "I would tell them God loves us. I would tell them he loves me too."

Thomas is still waiting for a sponsor. "He still has faith, but I am afraid for him," his mother said. "In too many ways, he is not like a child. Unless he can go to the Christian school, I will take him out of school next year. He must never, never lose his faith in God."

> **KEY BENEFIT: By giving a Sudanese child a Christian primary education, this donor gift allows that child a hope and a future.**
>
> **KEY CHALLENGE: Many of these children arrive at school traumatized. After primary school, many will face a strongly Islamic curriculum in secondary school.**

SPONSOR A CHILD: *China*

Out of the mountains they came. Little children—some as young as six, none more than twelve. They lived in some of the thousands of villages nestled on the mountainsides of southern China. From stark bamboo homes, without so much as a table or a chair, these children knew nothing of such conveniences as water pumps or electricity. None had access to medical care. The children made their way along steep, treacherous trails, carrying all the rice and beans and water they would need for two weeks. The trek took most of a day; some children would have to walk for six hours. But it was worth it. They were going to school.

In China, education is that important. Even the poorest of parents realize school is the key to escaping poverty. It's their children's only hope for a future.

But knowing it and paying for it are two different things. Although,

SPONSOR A CHILD

Begin a relationship that will change your life forever. Your gift provides tuition, school supplies, a uniform and, in some cases, a school lunch for a needy child. But best of all, it gives your child the opportunity to know the Lord Jesus Christ. A child is waiting for your help. . . . . . **$25/month or $300/year**

technically, education is free in China, so many fees are tacked on that many poor people simply cannot afford it. And if they are able to manage it, they send only their sons.

In the mountain villages, very few people have an income. Most are subsistence farmers who grow rice and corn to feed their families. Steep mountainsides are terraced so farmers can make use of every piece of their inhospitable land. But they cannot control the weather. The week before we arrived, a hailstorm had destroyed much of the corn crop. This meant many families wouldn't have enough to eat. Most likely, they would have to appeal to the government for help. It was that or starvation.

The only school in the area is in the town of Jia He. (The name can be translated "Abundant Harvest.") Because Jia He Primary School is many hours' walk from most villages, children live at the school for two weeks, then walk home to wash their clothes, visit their families for a couple of days, and get more food and water. When the weekend is over, they make the long, arduous trek back to school, carrying another two weeks' worth of supplies.

In 2003, a sudden flood washed away the Jia He Primary School. Even so, the principal refused to cancel classes. The children's education was too important. He insisted they meet in his house—all 120 students. The boys slept in the empty pigsty cubicles below the house, and the girls bunked in the loft over his father's house—for two entire years.

A church in Melbourne, Australia—which had been supporting some of the children in the school—raised the money to build a new school.

Partners International paid for bathrooms and a playground. And two years later, the children moved out of the principal's house and into their brand-new school.

In China, many rural schools are in extremely poor condition. The Chinese government not only accepts but actively solicits help in replacing these dilapidated buildings. Sometimes it allows the sponsoring organization (such as the church in Melbourne) to rename the school. When Jia He Primary School reopened, the sign above it read "Christ's Jia He Primary School," which means "Christ's Abundant Harvest Primary School." Today the new school is a constant reminder to the people of the area of Christ's love for them.

Through the local Chinese church, Partners International has introduced its Sponsor A Child program into many schools in southern China. Christ's Jia He Primary School is one of them. In fact, because of the poverty of the area, every single one of its 220 children needs financial help to attend school.

Although the program focuses on helping with educational fees, it doesn't always stop there. When the teachers described the treacherous trails along which the children walked—many narrow and rock-strewn, some infested with snakes—I gasped. "But that's so dangerous!"

"Well, it's not so bad now that the children have shoes," the teacher said. Yes, sometimes shoes and clothes are included in the program, as are other unique needs of a school—such as water.

WATER FOR LIFE

Not too many years ago, to get water, people in Jia He had to walk two hours each way. Many families took their children out of school simply because they needed them to carry water. It affected not only the children's education, but also their health. When a group came to the village and started a hygiene program, their cornerstone message was *Wash your hands!* The instructors couldn't understand why they were greeted by blank stares. Finally someone asked incredulously, "Why would we waste water washing our hands?" Only then did the instructors realize how precious water was there. They discontinued the class and went home.

That was before Partners International funded a reservoir for the village. One of the many positive effects was that school attendance jumped for village children, many of whom continued on through high school. Problem was, the reservoir was only big enough for village use. There wasn't enough water for the school too.

Since water was a particular need of the school, a new reservoir—strictly for the school's use—fell under the program's design. Soon children will no longer have to carry two weeks' worth of water along with them on their long walk from home.

On the side of the nearly completed reservoir hangs a sturdy metal sign that reads, in Chinese, "Christ is the spring of the water of life."

THE VILLAGE'S FUTURE

The junior high school is in a town farther away from the mountain villages. And the high school is farther still—another six-hour walk. Twelve hours for the most distant children. Yet most want to go on to junior high and even to high school. Many won't, but generally not because of the distance. Some will quit because their grades aren't good enough, others because of money. Even with help, 20 percent of the children cannot afford to go on to junior high, and half cannot afford high school. It is those who don't finish school, along with the old people, who will continue to farm the steep hillsides, constantly hoping for enough food to eat. Those who stay in school will leave.

Except for a few.

Liang Zhao Ming was born and raised in Jia He. While his friends and neighbors stopped going to school after junior high, he continued on through high school and then went to the Guangxi University in Nanning. Liang is the principal who kept the school going after the flood de-

Principal Liang with children from the village school (by Dan Kline)

stroyed the old building, who brought it to the new building and who continues to challenge the mountain children to be more than anyone else believes they can be.

With his education, Principal Liang could earn much more in a city school. And the working conditions would be far easier. (He had to leave his own home with the pigsty underneath because, like all the teachers in Jia He, he and his wife must live at the school.) But he is committed to the village. "I always intended to come back," he said. "This is where my heart is." His hope is that more of the children can go to high school and university, and that more will come back to the villages and help. Yet he knows that few are likely to do so.

Still his eyes glow when he speaks of the four or five children in each class who show special promise. It is those he watches over with special interest.

And there is the former student who is now at the university. "Do you think he will come back?" I asked.

"Maybe," Liang said. "All the time he was here, when I looked at him, I saw myself. Maybe he will."

WHAT GOD CAN DO

For many children throughout China, the Sponsor A Child program is a lifeline to which they can cling. And through the program, they can catch a glimpse of Christ—in the name on the school, in the sign on the reservoir.

"It's so great to see those kids in school," I said to Chong Lin, the translator who traveled with us. We were on the plane flying out of China, and mostly I was just thinking out loud. "I wish I could know the long-term outcome for these kids. Spiritually, I mean. I wonder—do you suppose any of them come to know Christ?"

"Yes," Lin answered in a voice so soft I barely heard her.

"What?" I asked.

"Yes. Some do come to know Christ."

"How do you know?" I asked.

"Because," Lin answered, "I was a sponsored child. And I did."

Just the year before, Lin told me, she had been talking to her pastor. One thing led to another, and she got out a picture of herself in first grade in which she held a placard with the number 381 on it. On the back of the picture, under the name and address of her school, was a brief sponsor description and child reference.

"Oh," her pastor said. "You were a sponsored child."

That was news to Lin. All her mother remembered was that Lin was a good student who got especially high marks in English, and the school assigned her a godmother from the States, which pleased her, because her family had five children and very little money for education.

"I remember getting gifts from America," Lin said. "And I got letters with nice stamps on the envelopes, which I gave to the boy who sat next to me because he asked me for them."

The year was 1968, and the sponsoring organization was—yes—Partners International. One of its donors had paid her school costs.

"Was your family Christian?" I asked.

"No," Lin said. "Not then."

After she graduated from high school, Lin had a real desire to go to church, but that wasn't an easy thing to do in China at the time. She didn't know anyone who was Christian. Finally she located a government church, which she attended every Sunday. And during the week, she prayed and read the Bible.

One elderly woman she met at the church made an especially strong impression. "She graduated from Bible school when she was eighty years old," Lin said. "That really inspired me, and I decided I wanted to go to Bible school too." And she did, attending for one year in Australia. Today almost everyone in Lin's family is a Christian.

What will happen in the life of a specific sponsored child? One you might sponsor, perhaps? Only God knows. But nothing is impossible.

By establishing Christian love in the community and gaining trust from the Chinese government, project workers are able to accomplish a great deal in the villages of southern China. The program also allows them to work closely with China's often-criticized open government churches—known as the Three Self Patriotic Movement. Much can be accomplished by partnering with those in the official church who have true faith and a heart to serve the needy in the name of Christ. It gives the Western partner access to an otherwise closed population, and it gives the church a great opportunity to witness.

One of the teachers at Christ's Jia He Primary School is from the church. "I'm sort of a missionary," she said. And that's not all. According to Jesus, "Whoever welcomes a little child like this in my name welcomes me" (Matthew 18:5).

> **KEY BENEFIT:** Chinese children gain the benefit of an education through this donor gift and are introduced to the loving, caring God.
>
> **KEY CHALLENGE:** Despite the claim of religious freedom, Christians working in China's atheistic public schools face many restrictions and challenges.

CARE FOR A STREET CHILD: *Senegal*

We were stopped in traffic in downtown Dakar, Senegal, when a little boy ran up and knocked on the car window. "Fifty cents," he called in broken English. "Only fifty cents." The boy held up a wire cage containing a dozen round balls of chirping, gray fluff, each with a bright red beak.

"Birds? Why would anyone want to buy those little birds?" I asked my host.

"Some people eat them," he said. "Others use them to make wishes."

The beggar boys, it seems, go out early in the morning and catch the birds, then they offer them for sale on the streets. I thought for a moment. Then I asked, "How much for all of them?"

"Five dollars," the boy said.

CARE FOR A STREET CHILD

Abandoned Senegalese children have no alternative but to beg for their food. Your gift provides one child with one month of nourishing meals and schooling, which will help change their outlook on life and make them more employable. They also learn about God's love through the Christians. **$40**

I gave the boy a five-dollar bill—American. Then I stepped out of the car and unlatched the cage. The birds hesitated, then one by one they fluttered out and up into the sky. Soon they were out of sight.

THE POWER OF THE MARABOUTS

Beggar boys are a common sight on the streets of Dakar. Most, however, aren't selling birds. Most are holding large tin cans and calling out, "Give, give, give in the name of God!" People drop money into their cans. Sometimes quite a lot of money. It's hard to believe, considering the look of the ragged, dirty boys with their wan and hungry faces. But the money isn't for them. It goes to their marabouts.

Marabouts are Islamic spiritual leaders unique to West Africa, especially urban Senegal. Hailed as saints and treated like celebrities, they are the ones who mainly control public opinion on religion and politics. Pictures of them are plastered all over Senegal—on bumper stickers and billboards, on the sides of taxis and buses, on posters in shop windows. These holy men—these experts in voodoo and potions and charms—are believed to stand between the people and God.

Many families, especially poor ones with many mouths to feed, give their sons to the marabouts, who use them as "holy beggars." Everywhere

A young boy out begging for his marabout (by Gulshan Lal)

one looks in Dakar—on the streets and sidewalks, ducking in and out of traffic, accosting pedestrians—these hollow-eyed boys dressed in rags are calling out for money in the name of God. There's no schooling for them; their life is on the street. Boys who don't collect enough money are punished at the end of the day. And at night, bone weary, they fall asleep huddled together in shacks.

They are, quite literally, slaves to their marabouts. Some will be slaves for life, providing free labor in the marabouts' fields when they grow too old to beg. With no education, those who do manage to get away face a bleak future.

Marabouts, on the other hand, are exceedingly rich. People are afraid not to give to one, for they believe that the marabout holds their very lives in his hands. And that he controls the next life as well, since he insists he has the power to pray them into paradise—or to have them barred for eternity. So in exchange for special access to God, poor parents continue to give away their sons, even though they know the boys will be treated badly. Even though they know their sons will pay the price all their lives. They consider it the cost of their own salvation.

Help for the Children

On a vast, sandy landscape dotted with knobby-armed baobab trees and clusters of thatched-roof huts stands a newly constructed dormitory. It's the main building in a center for abused and orphaned children.

It's not an easy region for Christian work. This is an area of Senegal known for the power and influence of the marabouts. Once when a marabout's car was stuck in traffic, his child-disciples made their way among the stopped vehicles and picked up his car. With him inside, they carried it to its destination. Allah forbid that the marabout be delayed by traffic.

And yet, despite the power of the marabouts, permission was given to build the Christian center, and street children continue to come. Some are orphaned and alone. Others were abandoned by parents too poor to support them. Still others escaped from their marabouts. Some are brought by desperate parents. When poor parents willingly bring their children to the center, they are told, "We are a Christian organization, and we will raise your children as Christians." The parents leave their little ones anyway.

Next to the dormitory, I spotted a small pit surrounded by neatly stacked cement blocks. Inside were two little tomato plants struggling to survive in the sandy soil. A boy came over and poured a glassful of water on them.

"It's just a start," the project leader told me. "But one day we will have an entire agricultural project here. Children will learn to grow vegetables. They will have plenty to eat, and any extras they can sell."

FROM MANY DIFFERENT DIRECTIONS

Not far away from the center for abused children, Carlos and Juanita— a missionary couple from Mexico—opened another compound for teenage street boys, many of whom had run away from marabouts. Every boy there is there by choice. Too bad the space is so limited, because many others are waiting for a chance to live at the compound.

Younger boys come to the center during the day, but there's no room for them to stay, so at night they go back to their marabouts. The small boys wistfully say, "When I'm thirteen . . . I hope . . . if there's room for me here . . ."

Besides a dormitory for the boys, the compound has a dining room and a church. Carlos and Juanita help the boys get jobs so they can make lives for themselves on their own. In fact, the couple bought and opened a restaurant in downtown Dakar for that very purpose. It's only open on weekends, and the boys, who work there five at a time, do everything— shop, cook, grill the meat, serve customers, clean up.

The idea is for the boys to earn their own money so they can buy their own clothes and pay for their personal needs. But the restaurant also allows them to learn a trade. Some boys even specialize. A teenager named Usman, for instance, makes great Brazilian coffee. A frequent visitor from Brazil brings the coffee beans, which Usman roasts and grinds. Three of the boys who work at the restaurant are now living on their own, fully self-supporting.

As we left the compound, a couple of boys ahead of us scampered up a tree. "What are they doing?" I asked.

"Catching birds," our host said. "They are always catching them. And there will always be someone to buy them. It may seem sad to you, but that's how it is. One person can't change it."

I thought about the dozen fluffy birds I had bought that morning, how they had flown away, safe and free. Maybe one person can't change the way it is. But one person did change it for them.

> **KEY BENEFIT:** This is an opportunity to cooperate with workers from other countries to redeem the lives of street children, transforming them from beggars and slaves into productive citizens with a future.
>
> **KEY CHALLENGE:** Marabouts have great power and influence in the area, and it is difficult to conduct a program that goes against their interests.

3

WATER OF LIFE

Okay, I'll admit it. When I first met Min Nareth, I was not impressed. He was . . . well . . . the best I can say about him is that he seemed downright glum. Even as he showed us his sleek white cow and her three calves, all the result of his participation in the local cow bank. Even when he pointed out his seven laughing children. Even when he nodded his consent to allow us up into the living quarters of his house on stilts. Everyone else was lounging in the hammocks below, waiting out the oppressive heat of the day, but he showed no interest in joining them.

Sighing deeply, Min climbed the stairs in front of us, then sat down on the thin bamboo slats that made up the upper floor of his home. I sat across from him, next to the car-battery-powered television set, and asked him questions with Pastor Sreeng acting as interpreter. Min responded with one-word answers. Never once did the hint of a smile touch his face.

Spying several neat stacks of books balanced on beams

WELL FOR A VILLAGE

Villagers are already grateful for the wells we have provided in Cambodia. But there are so many still in need. This practical, loving outreach helps prevent waterborne diseases, creates a community spirit and breaks down barriers to the gospel. . . . . **$460** above the family's sleeping mats, I asked, "What are those?"

Min said nothing, but Pastor Sreeng answered, "Hymn books and Bibles. Our church is right next door."

Through the window, I could see most of the village. It was much the same as most other Cambodian villages. Not a slum, certainly, but extremely poor. Sure enough, tucked in the grove of mango trees next to the house was a building with a wooden cross on top.

"Mr. Min let us build the church on his land," the pastor said. "Full use, for as long as we want it, free of charge."

"That's quite a gift." I took another look at Min's somber face.

"Yes," said Pastor Sreeng. "And that's not all he did."

QUEST FOR WATER

The River of Life Church Cambodia (RLCC) is a relatively new organization. Formed in 1996, its expressed goal is to make disciples of Jesus by planting churches throughout the country. And it's been quite successful. In just ten years, RLCC established over 150 churches scattered throughout Cambodia's twenty-three provinces. Today it is the largest church network in the country. The organization's plan is to establish a mother church in each province and develop it into a training center from which Christians can reach out to the villages within that province.

Although Cambodia now has freedom of religion, the government is still suspicious of Christianity. In the minds of the officials, it's just a Western religion. Certainly that's the position the government takes when Christians want to establish new churches. When those same churches reach out to meet the physical needs of the people, however, it's an entirely different matter. Then officials tend to look the other way and give the churches a lot more freedom.

"Mr. Min didn't think it was right for the church to sit empty throughout the week," Pastor Sreeng said. "He insisted it was a waste of God's house. So he arranged for school classes to be held there every day for the children in the area. We are teaching the children to read and write. It's the only school they have."

I looked at Min's impassive face. Smile or no smile, my impression of him was rapidly changing.

In Cambodia, all the churches are made up of, and run by, indigenous Cambodian Christians. Because the great majority of church members and leaders are themselves poor, they are quick to recognize the needs around them and to feel pain and want in a personal way.

One of the greatest needs is for a dependable supply of clean, accessible water. Much of Cambodia has always depended on the Mekong River. Every day, people in this area trek to the river to fill their water containers, then tote the water back home—water for drinking, water for bathing and washing clothes, water for the animals and the crops. All this water might well require many trips a day to the river and back again. It can mean a full-time job, especially for the children of the family, which doesn't leave much time for school.

As the river has grown more and more polluted, the rate of illnesses associated with drinking the water has climbed higher and higher. Babies and the elderly—the population's most vulnerable—are the ones hardest hit by waterborne diseases. The only way to make the river water safe to drink is to boil it thoroughly. But that takes time, patience and an understanding of the potential dangers. For much of the population, all of these are in short supply.

In times of drought, villages haven't been able to keep up with the need for water. Despite their best efforts, they have watched in despair as their crops withered and died. This is a desperate situation indeed, for most Cambodian families have no other way to bring in money. If they lose their crops, their families go without warm clothes, proper shelter and enough food to fill their stomachs. They have no alternate plan.

Water of Life

"If only we could build a well," church members said. "Not just for us, but for the entire village." What could be more appropriate than a gift of water from those who have the Water of Life?

With a well, villagers could irrigate their crops, which would mean they could produce a harvest even when there was no rain. And if church members could continue to have crops coming in, they would be able to continue to tithe their harvest, which would keep the church self-sufficient.

And so, three years ago, Min spoke up. He would make another gift, he said. This time he would give a piece of his land on the other side of the church, a place for the village to have a well. Right at that time, someone on the other side of the world picked up a gift catalog and determined, "Here's a gift I want to make. A well for a village in Cambodia."

Partners

When the well was finished, the church members and Pastor Sreeng gathered around to celebrate with David, Partners International's representative in the area. "What a great gift you gave us in this well!" they exclaimed to David.

"Oh, no," David said. "This wasn't just a gift. We were partners in this project. You did it with us."

"It costs much money to build a well," Pastor Sreeng said dubiously. "We don't have money."

"But Mr. Min donated the land," David said. "And every one of you contributed labor. You dug the well. In a partnership, each of us has a part to play. When we each faithfully play our part, we become equal partners."

The Cambodians stared blankly at David. In the Khmer language, there is no word for the concept of "equal partners." One person gives and the other accepts. That's just the way it is. Pointing to his feet, David said, "Both of my shoes walk in the dirt. Both are doing the same thing. My two shoes are slightly different, but is one better than the other? No. They work together to get me where I want to go. They are equal partners."

"Ah, I understand," said Pastor Sreeng. "Maybe you are right! Even though we have no money, we can be a partner in getting where we want to go."

JESUS LOVES ME WELL

Sometimes wisdom comes from the most unexpected places.

In a neighboring village, site of the first Cambodian well, someone had taken a stick and in the wet cement around the pump had scratched the words *Jesus Loves Me Well*. The wisdom in those simple words is so profound that it's now carved into the wet cement of every well a church

Jesus Loves Me Well (by Dan Kline)

constructs in Cambodia. It's a good reminder to the Christians. And for everyone else who comes for water, it's good news.

No, Min's demeanor never changed. Not once did I see the glimmer of a smile. Evidently he's just not the jovial type. But one thing is certain: by his actions Min is proclaiming, "Jesus loves me well"!

> **KEY BENEFIT:** This gift allows Cambodian churches to be involved in providing people with one of life's greatest necessities in the name of Jesus Christ.
>
> **KEY CHALLENGE:** Cambodian Christians lack confidence in their own ability to be partners in holistic work.

CLEAN WATER FOR A FAMILY: *North Africa*

Stunningly beautiful country stretched out before me, green and lush and dotted with gnarled olive trees. Steep hillsides, crisscrossed with corn standing tall in impossibly straight rows—especially considering men tended them using nothing but donkey-drawn hand plows—disappeared into the mist. So peaceful. Straight out of a storybook . . . until the putrid stench hit. Black water, Juan said. The very poor use it to fertilize their crops.

The very poor. Exactly the ones we had come to North Africa to see.

CLEAN WATER FOR A FAMILY

Water systems provide fresh water for Berbers and Arabs living in the mountains of North Africa. Women and children no longer have to walk several hours over mountain trails to fetch water. Your gift helps build a clean water system for a family and provides opportunities to share about God's love. . . . **$50**

We stopped close to the village school, and immediately, from nowhere, cheering children rushed forward to greet us—almost one hundred students with absolutely nothing to do. Only two teachers were available for the entire area, so this village school had classes just two days a week, from eight in the morning until eight in the evening. This was supposed to have been a school day. The kids showed up, but the teacher didn't, so they had nothing to do but follow along after us.

Laden with schoolbooks and lunches, and in some cases with baby brothers or sisters tied to their backs (with no one else to watch the little ones, the big kids brought them along to school), the children set off to show us the village pride and joy—the well.

THE VILLAGE WELL

We were in an ancient Berber village known as Eye of God. Just how ancient, no one seemed to know. What they did know was that the village well had always been in the same place. For centuries, it was nothing but a deep hole dug into the ground. Children would lean way over as they let down the rope on the water bucket, then they carefully drew up the water, one bucketful at a time, so they could fill their own water pots to carry home. Sometimes they were not as careful as they should have been. Far too many children fell down the well and drowned. Finally the villagers decided they had lost enough children, so they built a wall around the hole in the ground, and that's how it remained for the next several centuries.

The well had many problems: contamination by animals stepping over the wall and tromping around in the mud that then fell into the water; too little water in the dry season; easy access for those who lived close by, but a major problem for those farther away. Even so, nothing changed until donors looking through Partners International's gift catalog chose to make the gift of a new well to this village.

The water project was requested and conducted by PM International (PMI), a ministry that trains Latin American teams for crosscultural work in Muslim areas. Because PMI had already successfully developed over one hundred projects in this region, its workers knew how to proceed in a culturally sensitive way.

"When we want to work in a village, the first thing we do is go to the mayor, and he assigns us a bodyguard," said Juan. "Not to protect us, but to keep an eye on us. Strangers in a Berber village are not easily trusted. If we are to be accepted by them, it is important that we know this and that we honor it."

Of course, PMI would follow protocol. Cooperating with the officials is a given, as is working with the people.

Before PMI began the project, workers determined how much water the reservoir must hold to ensure that there would be enough for everyone, including the animals, in the middle of summer as well as when the rains were falling. Then, before the project could begin, PMI had to get signatures from 85 percent of the villagers indicating their approval. An important step, for even though the well was donated, the villagers would have to maintain the pump and the lines.

Collecting the signatures was no small task. House to house the workers went counting people and animals. Problem was, the people were always out working. So the PMI workers had to come back again and again and again. It took a tremendous amount of time. But it also allowed PMI workers to sit in the villagers' homes and talk with them. The two sides spent time together, sharing ideas and goals. PMI workers had an opportunity to suggest latrines for the school and a health education program. And through it all, the villagers and the workers got a chance to really get to know one another.

Today, in place of the deep and dangerous well hole, the village has a reservoir that holds enough water to last several months. Pulled up by a pump and carried through various pipes, the water is delivered directly into each house. For the first time, every one of the 112 village homes has running water. As does the mosque. And the school, by the way.

When all those children who swarmed around us that day grow up and tell their children stories about falling into the well and about the whole village getting sick because animals contaminated the water, the response will be, "Come on! Tell us a *true* story!"

THE IMPORTANCE OF RELATIONSHIPS

Despite the heat of the afternoon sun, I sat in an upstairs room shivering. It's amazing how cool those intricately painted tile walls can stay. Sinking back onto the overstuffed cushions, I sipped from my cup of freshly brewed mint tea.

"Come, enjoy the outside," Ferhat invited as he led me to the window. Ferhat, our host, was village president, the most important man in the area.

I gazed out at the cloudless azure sky, then down at the rolling hills of freshest green, dotted with acres and acres of trees in bloom. "The trees," I said, "what are they?"

"Almonds," Ferhat answered. "Eight thousand almond trees. All given to us by an international governmental organization." Eight thousand bearing almond trees. What a gift! Worth so much more than the donation of a single village well.

Ferhat smiled as though he read my mind. "Cost isn't everything," he said. Those trees were an amazing donation. Workers had arrived, planted them and then left within days. Packed up and moved on to the next project. They never sat in this room with the tile walls and sipped mint tea. Large governmental groups accomplish much, but they don't have time to go house to house to count people and animals or to talk over ideas while they wait for villagers to come home from the fields to sign their forms. They aren't able to call the children by name—or even the village president, for that matter. They simply don't have the time to develop relationships.

And without relationships, although they can do a huge amount of good, they cannot touch hearts.

Everyone agrees that water is vital. Everyone wants children to have latrines and better health. But when donors and recipients are coming from different places, and when the two cultures are so diverse, communication doesn't come easily.

"We don't impose anything on villagers," Juan explained. "Before we begin a project, they have to be convinced of what we're doing, of the benefits to them. If that happens, then we have communication."

As for Ferhat, he simply said, "I'm very thankful to God that we could have this cooperation. It is not easy to work with outsiders."

LIVING WELL PROJECT

Ferhat told me that, as a result of the water project, "We have a lot less disease, especially stomach problems. Also typhus. And not nearly so many babies are dying now." As a matter of fact, infant mortality in the village has been reduced by one-third.

The project would benefit both this generation and the next, Ferhat said, because a good well can keep going for many years. With a dependable water supply, villagers could raise more animals because they no longer had to worry about carrying them through the dry spells. And for the first time, villagers had felt secure enough to plant an entire grove of fruit trees. Already they were seeing the fruit beginning to set.

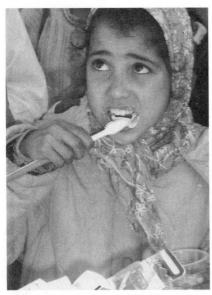

Water in the village means hygiene for the children (by Kay Strom)

Life in the village was changing. While the well is the centerpiece of the project, school latrines and the introduction of health education are also important innovations. But it will take a while for villagers to grasp the advantage of these.

"We appreciate the health education," Ferhat said diplomatically, "but it cannot benefit our children very much." The lesson of the day had been tooth brushing. Never before had the children seen a toothbrush. Each child was given one along with a tube of toothpaste. Then, after instructions, they all practiced brushing their teeth.

"Problem is," explained Juan, who teaches health education, "when the toothbrush is worn out and the toothpaste is gone, families don't have money to buy more."

"Maybe it will help future generations," Ferhat said.

Juan added, "We still do health projects, but we are paying attention to what the people say. And we're making changes to our program." This includes taking the lessons back to the basics: *Wash your hands before you eat.* "It sounds so simple, but people have never done it," Juan explained. "They come in from the fields, from working with the animals, then they sit down to eat with their hands. They never used to have water to spare, but now they do. So the challenge is to teach the children a new way while they're still young. Then when they grow up, it will seem natural to them."

BEYOND THE WELL TO THE WATER OF LIFE

Ninety-nine percent of the population in this area of North Africa is Muslim. Oil-rich countries in the Middle East pour huge amounts of money into the region in an effort to continue to strengthen Islam's role throughout the area—and, of course, to speed its push south through the continent. If the people of North Africa are ever to know the love of Christ, it will be because it is demonstrated to them in a culturally sensitive and appropriate way. It will be because love in action touches their hearts and lives.

This is one reason relationship building is so vitally important. For here is an important fact of the Muslim world: unless you initiate contact with their community and take the time and effort to form relationships and friendships, you cannot introduce people to the kingdom of God. It's next to impossible to pull a Muslim out of his or her community. But taking Muslims out of their communities is not the goal. The goal is to see God's fellowship built into that community, where it will flourish and grow.

As relationships are built between Christian workers and Muslims, the workers are able to talk naturally about their faith and, in a natural way, to share truths from the Bible. Ferhat was shown *The Jesus Film* and given a New Testament. His reaction? "The film was interesting. I enjoyed it. And I would like to keep talking about this man, Jesus."

North Africa is not a place where success is measured by churches established. It's a place where a well is built and a foundation of love is laid.

Soaud, a woman who lives near the village school, gets up early each morning to harvest vegetables from her new garden, then she sets out on her rounds—first to a poor widow woman, then to a family with many little mouths to feed, later to an elderly couple who have both been sick. "I saw how you were helping people, and I wanted to do the same," Soaud said to Juan. "You came here from very far away. I'm already right here. So, why don't I help my own people? That's what I thought."

Soaud was quiet for a few moments. Then she said, "What you are doing is planting in our minds to help people right here. It would be normal for me to stay at home and take care of my children. But I learned from you."

The lesson wasn't just from Juan. He simply carried it around the world to this remote mountain village in North Africa. It was initiated by someone who looked through a catalog and decided to reach out and donate a well.

KEY BENEFIT: North African Berber villagers gain all the benefits of a dependable water supply—along with school latrines and health education—and in the process they see Christ's love in action.

KEY CHALLENGE: In an area that has such an old and closed culture—and that is 99 percent Muslim—it is difficult and time consuming to develop the relationships necessary to build trust.

4

ENTERPRISING WOMEN

Any time the women's center was open, Meryem was there. She never missed a day. Or an opportunity. Meryem learned to type, then to use the computer. She made several baskets and a whole passel of photo frames, learned to weave intricate ribbon edging on towels (she made several sets) and hand painted a dozen magnets with elaborate scenes of North African landscapes. Meryem didn't want to miss out on anything.

After each meeting, while tea was being served, Meryem always managed to edge away from the other women and make her way over to Anita, the center's director. After a few comments about the project of the day, Meryem started in with the questions. Interesting questions. Thought provoking. And thoroughly unexpected.

"The hail that fell and destroyed so many crops last week," Meryem said one day, "do you think that was Allah's will, Anita?"

And another time: "Anissa's little girl is really sick. They're saying she

> **WOMEN'S SMALL BUSINESS START-UP AND TRAINING**
>
> Classes in sewing, computers and cooking bring village women together where they learn income-generating skills and have opportunities to learn about the message of Christ. Your gift provides items such as fabric and a shared sewing machine, a computer and printer, or pots and pans for one North African villager. **$130**

might die. It doesn't seem right that a little child should suffer so. Whose fault do you think it is, Anissa's or the child's?"

Such questions! Anita, a Christian from Argentina who worked in North Africa as a teacher, longed to grab onto them and explain God's sovereignty to Meryem. If only she could open the Bible and point to the answers Jesus gave when the same questions were posed to him. But Anita didn't dare. Not in North Africa. Not where the punishment for shaking the faith of a Muslim is so severe.

THE WOMEN'S CENTER

The North African National Women's Association Center where Anita works focuses on helping women who have few or no opportunities for an education. For the women who participate, it not only provides an incredible chance to learn new skills, but also vastly increases their likelihood of finding a job. At the same time, it builds their self-esteem and enhances their sense of dignity.

It's difficult to understand just how important the women's center is to Meryem and the other women who gather there twice a week. Life isn't easy for Berber women. And opportunities to get together and talk about ideas and possibilities, to express hopes and dreams . . . well, those are luxuries many never realize.

Work outside the home is the dream of many women. Some say it's their greatest need. But unemployment is a major problem in the area, and a great number of women cannot read and write. Few have more than four years of education. (Meryem was never allowed to attend school because there was no lavatory there, making it impossible for the girls to be modest.)

Employment training is a major thrust of the women's center, and it starts with literacy education. In the various skills seminars, women not only receive practical training, but also moral and emotional support that will help them as they move into the marketplace.

A special feature of the center is a computer-equipped lab. Women can attend classes to learn how to type and also how to use basic software programs. Because computers are usually too expensive for families to own, this lab opens the door to computer technology—a whole new world.

Another popular feature of the center is the library reading room, where books are available in Arabic, French, Spanish and English. It's an ideal place for women to study and for Spanish language classes too. Because a strong Spanish presence has long existed in this region of North Africa, many people already understand and speak the language, but becoming fluent makes women that much more employable.

Of course not all women can—or want to—work outside their homes. Learning to make handicrafts such as baskets, towels, photo frames or wall hangings offers them an opportunity to develop their own small businesses. They can make the items at home, then take them to the marketplace to sell.

A MINISTRY

Still, the women insist that the center is about much more than earning money. The most important thing, they say, is that they are finally able to get together and spend time with other women. In a country so closed to Christianity, this may well be the only opportunity for women to have their spiritual questions answered. "Developing their skills and seeing them get out of the house and be together is so good," said Anita. "But we also look forward to giving them the opportunity to hear the truth about God."

Yet the spiritual aspect must be handled with extreme care. As Anita listened to Meryem's questions, with their increasing spiritual bent, she weighed her answers carefully. Was Meryem asking generally, or did she want to know something specifically? Was she just airing personal curiosity, or did she have a sincere longing to know the true God?

Then one day Meryem stayed back until all the other women had left.

"Can we meet sometime, just you and me?" she asked Anita. After a moment of hesitation, she hastened to explain, "I'm not doing too well in my Spanish class. I thought maybe you could help me."

The next day, as Anita and Meryem sat together sipping mint tea at a quiet back table in a neighborhood café, with the Spanish text open before them, Meryem suddenly leaned forward and whispered urgently, "I had a dream a couple of nights ago about someone in a bright light. He was blindingly white, and he said he had a message for me. Anita, what does it mean?"

"I can't interpret dreams," Anita replied.

Anita took a long drink of her tea. Then after a deep breath, she ventured, "But I do know of a book that tells a lot about someone who sounds like what you're describing. And you know what? That person is right here with us now, Meryem, even though we can't see him."

Week after week, under the guise of studying Spanish, Meryem and Anita continued to meet at their quiet back table. Each time, they sat down and ordered tea, and Anita laid out the Spanish textbook. And each time, Meryem pulled out her latest list of questions. "What is the Trinity?" she asked.

"Who is Jesus Christ really?"

"What's the difference between Allah and the Christian God?"

"Is Jesus truly God's son?"

"Is it true that Jesus died on the cross?"

"Did he really come back to life again?"

Meryem learned very little Spanish, but she did come to know Jesus Christ. Anita gave her a Bible, which she read voraciously. Since she was unmarried and living alone, as long as Meryem was careful, it wasn't too difficult for her to keep her new faith a secret from her friends and family.

Then came the day of the wedding. One of Meryem's cousins was getting married, and the entire extended family flooded into town. Of course, they needed places to stay. While Meryem was away, some of the family came to her house and made themselves at home. As they were settling in, someone opened the closet in her bedroom, and off the top shelf tumbled her well-marked Bible.

For the first time in three years, Meryem didn't come to the women's center that week. Nor was she there the next week, nor the next, nor the next. "Her family was so furious they disowned her," the women whispered among themselves. "She has been cut off from all support. And she's been thrown out of her house. Who knows where she's living. Or how she's managing to eat."

Anita's heart fell. In North Africa, family is everything. Absolutely everything. Not only care and protection and emotional support, but physical support as well. What was Meryem going to do?

Several months passed, and Anita wasn't able to learn anything of Meryem's fate. Then suddenly one day Meryem appeared at the training center. "Can we meet for tea?" she asked Anita. "After classes today?"

Back at their old table, Meryem told Anita her parents had given her an ultimatum: Make a choice—Jesus or your family. "It was so hard," Meryem said. "But I finally told my family that if they forced me, I would choose Jesus. I told them I loved them so much, but . . ."

Against all sensibility, Meryem had made the choice to follow Christ.

"At first my parents turned me out and disowned me," she said. "They told me I would never see them again, that I was no longer their daughter. But then my mother contacted me and said they decided that the whole problem was that I needed to get married to a good Muslim husband. They had found one for me, and the wedding was set." It was not a suggestion, not a request. It was a command from her family. And so Meryem married Sidi.

"He doesn't know I'm a follower of Christ," Meryem said. "I don't dare tell him. Just imagine what he might do to me if he were to find out his wife is a Christian!" Yes. Under Shari'a law, he would have a right to do anything.

AND SO . . .

Local government officials praise the program offered by the women's center. They can't say enough about the difference it's making and the opportunities it's offering the women of the community. "We want to give women the chance to do new things," one official said. "They need ways to make money and improve their lives. We would like to see them add hygiene to the program."

"The woman is the root of the family," said another.

The women themselves praise the program too. "Before, we could do nothing. Now we can make something we can sell," said a beaming group of women. "We can make money. Also we feel useful and worthwhile."

As for Meryem, she continues to come for personal Spanish lessons, which is now an in-depth Bible study at the center. And she continues to grow.

Not long ago, Anita shared Meryem's story with a group of Christians working among the local people. "Sidi, you say?" asked Armando, a teacher from Brazil. "I've had some contact with a man named Sidi who just got married. He hasn't let me get into a serious talk with him yet, but he has asked me some interesting and probing spiritual questions." Could it be that Meryem's husband is also a secret believer? That he is as afraid to say anything to his wife as she is to him?

Meryem's story shows how God can use anything—including Spanish classes at the women's center—for his eternal purpose.

> **KEY BENEFIT: This gift allows uneducated and isolated women to build their educational skills, making them more employable as well as more personally and socially fulfilled.**
>
> **KEY CHALLENGE: Background, culture and Shari'a law all make it difficult to share the gospel with North African women, and those same things make it perilous for them to accept Christianity.**

SEWING MACHINE FOR A WOMAN: *Senegal*

"I never went to school," Assana explained half-apologetically. "I can't read or write in French. It's too hard. But that's all right, because I conduct my business in the Wolof language. I learned to read and write in Wolof here while I was learning to sew."

If the sewing classes in Dakar needed a poster girl, they wouldn't have to look any further than Assana. Six years ago, she was a typical wife in Senegal's capital city. Her husband worked, but the meager wages he brought home couldn't adequately feed and clothe their family of seven. Assana wanted to help, but she was illiterate. What could she possibly do to bring money into the family? So she kept herself busy cooking and cleaning and worrying about the future. Her two sons went to school for a couple of years, just long enough to learn the basics. But her daughters? The idea of them in school never even occurred to Assana.

It was Assana's neighbor who told her about the sewing course. "It takes three years to finish the entire course," she said, "but after that, you can start your own business and really make some money."

> ### SEWING MACHINE FOR A WOMAN
>
> In cities, villages and refugee camps where electricity is expensive, unreliable or nonexistent, foot-pedaled sewing machines allow women to make a living for their family. Your gift provides a woman in Mali, Senegal or Sudan with a way to earn money and gives her a valuable ingredient for life— hope! $250

"But . . . I can't," Assana stammered.

"Read and write?" said her neighbor. "Don't worry. They teach you there. In Wolof. You don't have to learn French."

When Assana heard that the course would cost her fifty dollars a year to help pay for the fabric and other materials, she almost gave up on the idea. But her husband said, "We will borrow the money. Just think of

Assana models her sewing success (by Kay Strom)

how much you will be able to earn when you finish the course!"

During the first year, Assana learned basic reading, writing and simple math, and she learned to sew by hand. She made towels and linens, which she carefully decorated. This alone was a nice trade, and some of her classmates went no further. But Assana also tried out the treadle sewing machine (electricity was too undependable to use electric machines), and she knew she would never be happy simply sewing by hand. The second year, she began to sew baby blankets and skirts on the machine. The women who stopped at this level were seamstresses. But to be a tailor, she needed the third year.

By the time she finished, Assana was able to design and make her own dresses; she sold two she made while she was still in school. She could also make men's suits. And she could read and write just as if she had gone to school. She could even keep her own business books. "See?" her proud husband said. "I told you we would make the money back!"

THE IMPORTANCE OF MICROENTERPRISE PROGRAMS

More than three billion people live on less than two dollars a day. Many of the catalogs I collected had donor options that could benefit impoverished families by helping them gain financial independence through small businesses. Heifer International focuses solely on giving families the opportunity to raise animals for this purpose—everything from camels and water buffalo, to cows and chickens, to honeybees.

World Vision considers microenterprise to be one of their hallmark development programs. "We may be their last option," the organization's representative said. "Traditional banks make it difficult for the poor to get a loan."

For every organization, most loan recipients are women. Research shows that they are the most reliable at paying loans back. Also, as World Vision points out, "the impact of the loans on the women and children is extraordinary."

THIS PROGRAM

Sewing is only one part of the program Inter-Senegal Mission has been operating together with Partners International since 1995. Besides training women in sewing and tailoring, it teaches them to bake cakes and make pastries and cookies to sell. The goal for women such as Assana is not only to learn a skill but also to become literate and to learn to conduct a business. Only then will they be able to bring badly needed money into their families.

Everyone who goes to the sewing school knows that Christians run it. Senegal, over 90 percent Muslim, is dominated by wealthy and powerful Islamic brotherhoods. Although the Senegalese government prides itself on religious tolerance, as in most Islamic cultures, it is extremely difficult to openly share one's Christian faith. This is why it's so important that the love of Christ be shown in action.

While the majority of the students and even much of the staff are Muslim, the school has a sprinkling of Christians. But because of the social cost of following Christ, some are secret believers. Consider twenty-two-year-old Ida, for instance. She has been at the school for five years, first as a student and now as an instructor. Ida lives with her uncle and aunt, two brothers and three cousins. For three years she has been a follower of Christ, yet she dare not tell her family. "My uncle would throw me out, and I have nowhere to go," she said. "My entire family would disown me. What would I do without my family?"

"We cannot make decisions for Ida," said Monica, the young woman from Costa Rica who heads up the sewing program. "How can any one of us say what we would do in such a situation? It is very, very difficult for them. But we continue to work with Ida, and we study the Bible with her. And we pray for wisdom and strength for her."

A BIG DREAM

From the beginning, Assana's big dream was to own a sewing machine. But of course, that was nothing more than a dream. She knew how much it would cost—more money than she had ever seen in her life. Then she had a class in school that gave her instruction on how to save money. It was a totally new concept. Saving isn't a part of her culture. Who ever had anything extra to save, anyway? Still, Assana determined she would do it.

"I try to save money, but it's so hard!" Assana said. "I just don't have enough. What can I do, tell my children not to eat?" And yet she was most impressed by the benefits of saving. Maybe, just maybe, the sewing machine could be more than an impossible dream. She did manage to save fifteen dollars, but then her son needed the money in order to go to school. Another time she saved twenty-five, but her husband got hurt and couldn't work for a month, so she had to use it to buy food for the family. Still she was determined. So once again, she started putting money away.

HEARING ABOUT GOD

When Assana finished her three years of schooling, Monica gave her a special award for all she had accomplished. But Assana knew the truth:

There just wasn't much she could do without a sewing machine.

"Why don't you teach at the school?" Monica asked. And for the past several years, that's what Assana has been doing. Teaching first-year sewing—and saving her money.

Every morning, Monica leads devotions for the staff of the sewing school. Although not all the workers are Christians, all must be willing to listen. Assana never minded. In fact, she looked forward to it. And when she heard about the two Muslim Bible study groups Monica was leading, Assana immediately asked to join them both. Any lively discussion, she wants to be there. Like most Senegalese, Assana is religious and wants to know more about God. And with fifty people in the study, she really enjoys the fellowship.

"Muslims especially want to know about the prophets," Monica said, "so that's where we start in the Bible studies—where everyone is in agreement. Then we move on to the New Testament."

At first Assana didn't say much in the study groups. She just listened. Now that she feels more comfortable, she is beginning to ask questions.

NOTHING IS IMPOSSIBLE . . .

One day, Assana came home from the sewing school, and as usual her sixteen-year-old daughter, Fatima, was cooking dinner and cleaning. "Is this what I will do for my whole life?" Fatima asked her mother.

No, Assana determined. It was not. "Why don't you come to the school with me?" she said. "You can learn to read and write too. Then you can decide what kind of business you want to do."

Assana and Fatima. Mother and daughter. They were an exciting first for the sewing school. Poster girl and second generation. Teacher and first-year student.

Oh, about the sewing machine. Assana had saved fifty-two dollars, and then her mother fell ill. Between the cost of the doctor and the hospital, it not only took all her savings, it also left her in debt. Assana went back to the school and asked Monica, "Would it be possible for me to stay late and use the sewing machine here? I now understand that I will never be able to save enough to buy my own."

"No," said Monica. "We've had to make a rule that we would not allow that. There are too many who would want to use our machines, and we cannot possibly accommodate them all." The smile slipped from Assana's face, and she turned to go.

"But Assana . . ." Monica said.

"Yes?"

"Someone in America sent in a donation for a sewing machine. Just yesterday we decided that it should go to you. Congratulations."

KEY BENEFIT: After a woman has completed a sewing course, the gift of a foot-pedal sewing machine provides her with one of the surest ways to escape poverty and make a living for her family.

KEY CHALLENGE: The high cost of a sewing machine makes it extremely difficult for a woman to get one on her own.

WOMEN'S SMALL BUSINESS START-UP: *India*

For as long as she could remember, Jagrity had labored in her landlord's fields. She was just a young girl when she started trudging out at dawn with her mother and father. When she was thirteen, her father arranged a marriage for her, and from then on, she accompanied her husband, Kumar, to the fields every day. Jagrity got up before it was light to prepare the kitchen fire and cook the rice so that she could be at work by the time the sun came up. The other housework would wait until she came back after dark. In the scorching midday sun of India's hot season, she worked in the fields. And in the driving rain of the monsoons, she worked in the fields. Jagrity was in the fields the day her first child was born, and that's where she was at the birth of her second and third and fourth babies.

Every month Kumar went to the landlord's office to get an accounting of the family debt. The landlord took out his account book and consulted his notes and figures. Kumar was free to check them, the

WOMEN'S SMALL BUSINESS START-UP

A long drought and inflation make it almost impossible for many villagers in rural India to provide for their families. Your gift will train a woman in an income-generating trade such as handicrafts, mushroom growing or pickle making. Your gift will also provide her with the funds to start her own business. . . **$100**

landlord said, but they both knew Kumar couldn't read, so the landlord read it to him. It was always the same. No matter how hard Jagrity and Kumar worked, no matter that their twelve-year-old son had started working alongside them, the landlord always announced that his figures showed their debt was growing larger. They lived in a house on the landlord's land. They ate the landlord's rice. What choice did Kumar have? It was always the same; Kumar bowed his head and sealed his consent with his thumbprint.

Work. Weariness. One hard day after another. It's all Jagrity had ever known. Never once did it occur to her that anything could be different.

Like nearly one-third of India's staggering billion-plus population, Jagrity and Kumar are Dalits—untouchables. As members of India's lowest social caste, they suffer cruel discrimination and economic hardship. Little wonder that so many Dalits carry a deep-seated sense of hopelessness and inferiority. It's been pounded into them by countless generations of oppression and prejudice.

Then came the great drought. Fewer and fewer crops grew, which meant less and less work for Jagrity and Kumar. The landlord wouldn't let their son work at all. And he gave the family less rice to eat. As the drought worsened, the landlord wouldn't let Jagrity in the fields either.

The family's rice allotment became smaller still. Kumar and the boys ate most of it. Almost none was left for Jagrity and the girls.

Then came the day when the landlord told Kumar, "I have no more work for you. Take your family and be off my land by tomorrow." What were Kumar and Jagrity to do? Laboring in the fields was all they had ever known. And now the fields were bare.

They moved to a nearby village, where Kumar managed to find a few hours of work each day. But he also found solace in alcohol. And Jagrity, despised and illiterate, was left with starving children and absolutely no way to feed them.

FROM DESPERATION TO HOPE

Often Dalit women are called "Dalits of the Dalits." Considered doubly inferior by the Hindu majority since they're not only from the lowest caste but also women, they have it especially hard. Far too often Dalit women fall victim to the evil socioeconomic practices that prevail in India's caste-oriented society. Few have the chance to get an education. And employment opportunities are almost nonexistent for them. Add to this that they are raised to feel worthless.

Worthless is exactly how Jagrity felt as she watched her life slipping away. And when she looked at her children, she saw nothing but hopelessness and despair.

But Jagrity was more fortunate than most. Her new village, at the southern tip of India, was close to the women's center run by Bible Faith Mission (BFM). Dalit-run BFM works to bring economic, social and spiritual transformation to the Dalits through holistic projects.

Invited to the center by a neighbor, Jagrity was amazed at the array of handicrafts on display. Other women had made the lovely things and were taking them to the market to sell. Poor Dalit women—just like her! There were woven mats and baskets, and lotions and creamy soaps made from coconut oil, and beautifully colored candles, and all sorts of hand-stitched linens and tablecloths, and clothes and purses. To her astonishment, she even saw homemade pickles and vegetables women had grown in their own gardens behind their houses.

"But I don't know how to do any of these things," Jagrity said sadly to her neighbor. She was told that people at the center could teach her.

"But I couldn't have a business because I can't read or write," Jagrity confessed. People would teach her that as well.

"But I have no money to buy the things I need to start," she said. She could get a loan, her neighbor told her. There are people on the other side of the world who have faith in Dalit women and want to see them succeed. People who are willing to help.

"I don't know if my husband would sign for a loan," Jagrity said sadly. It wouldn't be his loan. It would be *her* loan. The business would be hers, just hers.

Jagrity had no more questions. It didn't seem possible, yet her family desperately needed money. And if there was a chance . . .

WOMEN—THE HOPE

I first met Jagrity at a market fair at BFM's women's center. That day the room was filled with tables on which beautiful items were displayed—everything from toys to pickles, from jewelry boxes to fine soaps. Jagrity was standing behind her group's display of woven mats and baskets, and intricately embroidered linens and tablecloths.

I stopped to pick up one of the mats. "Wow!" I said. "What a lot of work to make something like this!"

"I could teach you," Jagrity said with a shy smile. "Do you want to try?"

Now it was my turn to be shy. It looked awfully complicated to me, and I told her so. Jagrity gathered an armload of reeds, then she settled herself on the ground outside and extended one leg. I watched as she wound long reeds around her big toe then pulled the two ends of the reeds taut. More quickly than I could follow, her fingers darted back and forth, back and forth, back and forth. Sure enough, a sturdy, intricately woven pattern began to emerge.

As Jagrity tied off the finished piece, she said, "Now, you try it." I sat

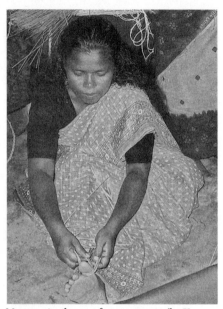

down, extended my leg and did my best to tie the reeds around my toe. As Jagrity helped, I pulled the two ends as tightly as I could. But as soon as I tried to weave the reeds in, the whole thing fell apart.

"I guess it's just something I can do," Jagrity said with a big grin. "I can do many things now." She really can. One of the things Jagrity can do is conduct her own microenterprise in a truly businesslike manner. BFM made certain that she

Mat-weaving lessons from an expert (by Kay Strom)

had the proper training. That's one of the reasons the women have a perfect payback record on their loans.

When Jagrity first got her loan, she rode the bus all day to an area where she could buy reeds to make mats. Traditional in many homes, the mats were familiar to her, and she already knew how to weave them. Also, the supplies were relatively inexpensive, even though getting them was inconvenient and time consuming.

"Many women chose to make mats for the same reasons," the BFM director told me. "But then they couldn't sell them. Too many are available at the market and not nearly so many people use them anymore. Even when they do sell, they don't bring in much money." So now the mats are made only as a sideline. For her business, Jagrity was encouraged to start decorative stitchery, an art that is especially lucrative.

As I walked through the room, inspecting the wide variety of fine goods the women had for sale, the impact of the program was obvious. But never so much as when I looked at Jagrity.

Before she went to the women's center, no one ever told Jagrity that she had a life of worth. Knowing this has given her a passion to reach out to other women. She wants them to understand their true value too, and their ultimate purpose.

KEY BENEFIT: Dalit women have an opportunity to gain financial security and a sense of self-worth through building a microenterprise. This project not only provides a loan, it also ensures that women learn to organize and manage their businesses.

KEY CHALLENGE: Many Dalit women suffer from a deeply ingrained sense of worthlessness and hopelessness. Also, it is vital that the specific product first be determined to fill a need in the marketplace.

5

IS THERE A DOCTOR IN THE HOUSE?

"Let's see, here is a school . . . and over there is a reservoir," I said as I looked around the village high in the mountains of southern China. "What about a clinic? Do you have any medical care up here?"

No, I was told. No clinic, no doctor, no nurse. The closest medical facility of any kind was two hours away by car. Trouble was, no one had a car.

"What happens when someone is sick?" I asked.

The clinic sends their car twice a week, I was told. Whenever someone is sick or hurt, they wait for the car, and it takes them to the medical facility for treatment.

"But," I said, "what happens when someone gets really sick—or badly hurt—and it isn't one of the days when the car comes? What then?"

In that case, I was informed, the person simply suffers until the day the car comes. Or they get well while they wait. Or else . . . they don't. Like the little boy who was bitten by a snake on his way to school. It happened the day after the

MEDICAL CLINIC

Most people living in China's villages must travel hours to see a doctor, and often they aren't well enough to make the trip. Your gift will build and equip a medical clinic to treat the sick and serve as a positive Christian witness. Any amount toward a clinic will help. **$6,600**
(or any contribution)

clinic car came, so he had to wait in anguish for four days. He died the night before the car arrived.

"Someday we will have our own clinic right here," the headman of the village said. "It will be a place of help for us, just like the school. And like the school, it will be a place where people from the smaller villages can also come for help. Someday, maybe."

THE SITUATION AS IT IS

Sad, to be sure, but not a unique situation. Many poor rural Chinese villagers have no access to health care. The problem is, doctors and hospitals are largely concentrated in China's large cities. Yet the southernmost part of the country is dotted with many thousands of small villages, most of which have no access to medical help.

To make matters worse, most mountain villages—especially those in the high regions of Guangxi and Guizhou provinces—are connected by steep, twisting dirt roads that sometimes are little more than trails. No public transportation exists there. Even in the best of conditions, it often means a day's journey by donkey cart or on foot to get to a medical clinic in a nearby town. And in the rainy season, the roads are often impassable.

Little wonder, then, that most villagers don't even consider health care an option. Herbs, poultices, home remedies and good-luck charms—when illness strikes, these are all they have to rely on.

Certainly no one questions the value of village clinics, and medical outposts have been established in certain villages. Yet many of these are in run-down buildings—dirty and unsafe, totally unfit for medical care. The Chinese government recognizes the problem. In a unique move, it's asking for assistance in upgrading these poorly maintained clinics. Since Christian groups have shown a willingness to help, the government has demonstrated an unexpected willingness to make surprising allowances to them.

CHRIST'S FAITH, HOPE AND LOVE MEDICAL CLINIC

In exchange for help in rebuilding the dilapidated clinics, the local government has agreed to name them Christ's Faith, Hope and Love Medical Clinics. Pretty amazing in a soundly atheistic country. Even more surprising, the government will permit the clinics to have an indirect Christian influence. For instance, Christian literature can be laid out in prominent places.

In some regions, Chinese churches are closely linked with the medical clinics. Some have even taken over the management. Partners International determines where it will place its clinics on two criteria: an area's need for medical aid and the presence of a local pastor who faithfully teaches the gospel and can follow up in the village. All this is done with the full support of the Chinese government.

The next day we left the city and drove for several hours, first on the main road, then far up a rutted dirt road, until we finally reached another dusty mountain village. Our driver parked under a clump of tangled trees. "See that building?" the translator said, pointing to a rundown shack. "That was the old clinic. It was established there more than thirty years ago." Then she pointed across the road to the new building. "That's the new clinic. It moved last year."

Over the door of the attractive storefront was a red cross, and above that, in Chinese letters, Christ's Faith, Hope and Love Medical Clinic. Double doors hung wide open. Just inside stood two large glass cases filled with neatly stacked first-aid materials, over-the-counter treatments and prescription medications.

From the back examination room, Dr. Wong nodded. She adjusted the blanket on a woman lying on the bed, then came to greet us. "Come, let's talk," Dr. Wong said through the translator.

As we sat together on a bench out in front, curious villagers gathered around to stare—children, elders, young men on their motorbikes. Evidently we were the most interesting thing that had happened in quite a while.

By Chinese mountain standards, this was actually a large village—over seven hundred families, Dr. Wong told us. People also came in from the surrounding areas for medical care. She estimated that she saw about a dozen patients each day. She also went to the hospital daily, which is about twenty minutes away by car.

As we talked, an elderly woman stepped forward and spoke in a soft voice. "She wants to tell you that she had a fever and Dr. Wong made it go away," the translator said.

The woman grabbed a little boy by the hand and pulled him forward. "He had the flu," said the translator. "She says Dr. Wong gave him a wonderful medicine, and he was well the next day. The very next day!"

Then many people were talking at once. Everyone seemed to have a story of an illness or an injury, and of Dr. Wong and her wonder drugs. "Stomach problems," the translator said. "Lots of them said they had stomach problems. She's good at fixing that."

Something the people didn't seem to realize was that the village was actually experiencing far less illness than it had in the past, because Dr. Wong was especially active in preventive work. "I go to all the primary schools in the area to talk about hygiene and how to keep from getting sick," she said.

A Doctor in the Village

The village is fortunate to have Dr. Wong. She grew up right there, among those very families. As a child, she went to the old clinic and was treated by the old doctor. By the time she started junior high school, she had already determined that she would be a doctor and that she would stay in the area and provide medical services to her own people. "I knew it was important for me to do this," she said, "because people here are too far away from other medical help."

After she finished high school, Dr. Wong spent two years training with the old doctor, following and watching, and learning all she could from him. Her only regret is that she doesn't have more formal medical training. "I can tell people some things," she said, "but I really don't feel well enough qualified. I wish I could go to medical school and become a real certified doctor. But I know there isn't much chance I'll ever be able to do that."

"Tell about your daughter," a young man on a motorbike urged.

Dr. Wong's eyes lit up, and her face broke into a proud smile. "She's in the city, in medical school," she said.

The city is a big lure for village young people. Some go to school; some find jobs; some get married. But few ever come back to the villages, especially not after receiving medical training. Not after seeing the working conditions the city has to offer and the array of modern medical equipment available to city doctors. Not when they know the amount of money they can earn there. Why return to the harsh life back home?

Evidently Dr. Wong knew what I was thinking, because she said, "I do think my daughter will come back and take over for me here." After a pause she added, "I hope so. I really hope so."

COUNTING THE COST

It costs approximately $6,600 to rebuild a rundown medical clinic in China, to outfit it with the necessary medical equipment and to furnish the initial supply of medicines. That's a pretty hefty chunk of change, to be sure. But many donors choose to give a smaller donation, then the gifts can be combined to fund a clinic. The local government covers the basic salary of medics such as Dr. Wong. Also, since patients pay for their own medications, the cases of medicines are constantly replenished. Yet poverty-stricken patients are never turned away. Partners International makes certain that anyone who comes to the clinic in need of medicine will receive help, regardless of whether or not she or he is able to pay.

"So," I asked Dr. Wong, "what is the biggest change you have seen in your time at this clinic?"

She didn't even need time to think. "People are more open to new things," she said. "Hygiene, vaccinations—it's all new to them, but they listen and they are willing to change."

Mostly, of course, they are willing to change because of Dr. Wong. Not only does she go to the schools, but she also visits with each family in the village. She sits with them in their homes, listens and talks with them about their concerns, explains how simple hygiene can help keep their children well. Then she demonstrates her concern by following up on each family to see how they are doing. Not something that would—or could—come from a big-city hospital!

KEY BENEFIT: The gift of a medical clinic—or a donation toward one—gives Chinese villagers access to badly needed medical care, all in cooperation with, and with support from, the Chinese government. Because it is done in conjunction with local Chinese churches, people can also be ministered to spiritually.

KEY CHALLENGE: Finding doctors to work in these outpost village clinics.

Prenatal Follow-up and Care: *Senegal*

It was a sweltering Sunday in Senegal, and the morning church service had been close to three hours long. But instead of pronouncing the benediction, the pastor announced that we were about to be part of special celebration. A *ngente*—a baby-naming ceremony—is traditionally held on the eighth day after a baby's birth, but this baby's father had decided to wait for a month, just to be certain his little one survived (his previous two had not).

This was no traditional *ngente,* where a Muslim marabout gives the baby a name and a blessing. Instead it had much of the flavor of a Christian baby dedication.

Rachel. That's the name the father chose for his daughter.

Music played. Children danced and sang. The congregation joined in with great enthusiasm. Then the mother danced up to the front, holding baby Rachel high in the air. Behind her came another woman, and the mother handed Rachel to her. Then came another woman, then another, then another. As each came up, the woman before passed the baby along to the next woman. "What are they doing?" I asked the man next to me.

"Oh, they're establishing the order of who would raise the baby if something should happen to her mother," he said.

PRENATAL AND FOLLOW-UP CARE

With no medical care available in many Senegalese villages, childbirth is dangerous—sometimes taking the life of a mother or her baby. Your gift provides three prenatal visits, at least two anti-tetanus vaccines for an expectant mother and postnatal care for the baby. **$37**

After much singing and dancing, and after the procession of eight women, the *ngente* ended with prayer. First the father, then the pastor, thanked God for the nurse who helped ensure that mother and child both survived. Then they asked God's protection for little Rachel as she grew and that he would grant life and health to her parents so they could raise her to know him.

SENEGAL'S HEALTH CARE

In Senegal, the survival of mothers and babies is not taken for granted the way it is in the developed world. The country's maternal mortality ratio is almost 500 deaths for every 100,000 live births (in the United States, the ratio is 7 maternal deaths for every 100,000 live births). In rural areas, where a woman's social status remains closely tied to her role as a mother, women give birth to an average of five or six children. With each child, her chance of dying increases. In many parts of rural Africa, one in nineteen women dies as a result of pregnancy or childbirth.

Thanks to prenatal and postnatal medical care provided through the gift of a caring donor, Rachel's mother had a far better chance of beating those dismal odds. Alima has a different story.

Alima shuddered as she recalled the birth of her baby. When complications became unbearable, she was packed into a donkey cart and for almost forty miles she bounced over hot, dusty dirt roads before finally reaching a clinic. "I was actually hoping I *would* die," she recalled with a grimace.

Quite simply, Senegal's health-care system is not able to provide proper care to poor and rural communities. Malaria and malnutrition abound. Anemia, meningitis and polio are far too common. Severe health problems caused by parasite-contaminated water and food run rampant. For the vast majority of mothers-to-be, prenatal care is unheard of. And follow-up care for babies is nonexistent.

Medical care is one of rural Senegal's greatest needs. For expectant mothers and newborn babies, it can mean the difference between life and death.

When a small medical center opened in a rented house in a poor section of the city of Thies in 1999, a medical work began that was to reach out to the surrounding villages in many different ways. Five years later, assisted by Partners International, the newly named Barthimee Medical Center moved into a new four-story building. In addition to basic medical care and general consultations, it offers vaccinations, dental care (a real luxury in Senegal), lab analysis and nutritional counseling. It also offers prenatal consultations and well-baby care. In 2004, about 18,500 people were seen there.

But that's not all. The medical center also reaches out to the surrounding villages so badly in need of medical care. In 2004, through mobile medical teams, the center assisted another 14,000 people.

When I visited Barthimee Medical Center, the third floor had just been completed. Dr. Ray, the surgeon, was busily cleaning and disinfecting the operating room that Partners International donors had outfitted

92 HARVEST OF HOPE

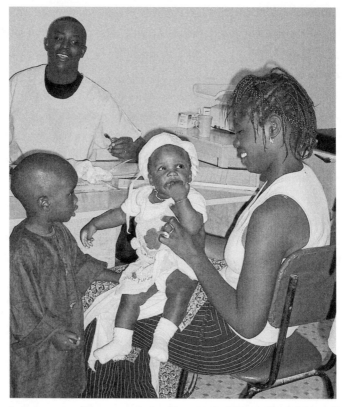

Patients get excellent care at the Barthimee Medical Center (by Gulshan Lal)

so generously and so completely. At last the medical team would be able to help with complicated pregnancy cases requiring such interventions as Caesarean sections.

"We go slowly," Dr. Ray said. "If we don't rush in and try to do things we're not totally set up to do, then we'll be safe and have good standards, and we'll be a blessing to the community."

Without a doubt, the medical work has grown. It now includes a skilled Senegalese medical staff. But the need has also grown, especially in villages where people have no doctor. Resources must reach out from Barthimee Medical Center into those areas. It's vital that the clinic continue to establish small village clinics in rural areas. At highest priority is finding ways to reduce the deaths of new mothers and their babies.

No more Alimas should have to travel for hours in agony in the back of a donkey cart. Many more Rachels should have their healthy births celebrated.

SPIRITUAL CONNECTION

Senegal is made up of a number of people groups. Inter-Senegal Mission, the first indigenous church-planting agency in Senegal, is working to spread the good news of Jesus Christ to the country's rural villages, specifically to the Wolof and Serer people. Working through holistic projects, such as providing medical resources and prenatal clinics, it builds relationships while providing badly needed medical care. This compassionate work touches lives in a very real way. "When Jesus was on earth," one donor said, "his ministering always seemed to be preceded by healing the sick and relieving the suffering around him. Only then did he speak of spiritual truths. If I want to follow Christ, I feel I would do well to consider following that pattern."

At baby Rachel's dedication, the pastor prayed, "We give thanks to God that this precious baby is alive. And that her mother is here to raise her in the ways of God." How much we take for granted. How much a thirty-seven-dollar donation can do!

KEY BENEFIT: Prenatal care for expectant women, and follow-up care and vaccinations for their babies, help to lower the incredibly high rate of deaths among women during childbirth and their newborn babies.

KEY CHALLENGE: Many rural villages have no access to medical care other than medical teams sent out from Barthimee Medical Center.

Medicine for a Poor Family and Gifts-in-Kind Medicines: *Africa*

Some gift opportunities are ready-made for donor appeal: A tiny child, with twig-thin limbs and huge, haunting eyes that stare straight into your heart. Buy him a healthy today and a hopeful tomorrow, and it will set you back only thirty dollars a month. Other opportunities are, to be perfectly frank, a hard sell: A crateful of medical materials shipped to a hospital in Africa for only—gulp!—twelve thousand dollars.

How many for the sweet little child with the heart-rending eyes?

Okay, who's in line for the crate?

That's what I thought. But heart appeal isn't always the best way for an individual donor to determine the wisest investment. That little one needs a sponsor to be sure, but don't be too quick to shrug off the crate.

> **MEDICINE FOR A POOR FAMILY**
>
> In Liberia and Sudan, wars have destroyed most of the health facilities. In many sub-Saharan villages of Senegal, people have no access to medical treatment, not even to an aspirin. The child mortality rate runs high. Your gift will provide medicine for a poor African family. **$8**

Consider Dr. Ray, looking out in despair over a crowded waiting room (an average of one hundred men, women and children pass through each day). He knows that the people packed in there are only a fraction of the sick and needy in this part of Senegal. But, what's he to do?

There's the stomach-cramping-hungry mama fretting over her two malnourished little ones, both dying from malaria. So sad. Dr. Ray could treat them all with good results—if only he had the medicine. And that woman with the deep cough, and the man on the other side of the room leaning against the wall because he can no longer sit up—they both have pneumonia. But there's no penicillin to give them. From different corners of the room come moans of agony—a badly infected tooth here, a broken arm over there, in the corner, a gash in the leg. But Dr. Ray has no painkillers to relieve their suffering. Medicines and medical equipment are extremely hard to come by in the area. And even when they can be found, the cost puts them way out of reach of people such as these.

GIFTS-IN-KIND MEDICINES

In Senegal, Sudan and Liberia, waterborne disease is prevalent, but medicine is not. Through our Gifts-in-Kind program, we provide Christian doctors and clinics with desperately needed medicines, medical supplies and medical equipment. Your investment of $12,000 purchases these items valued at up to $750,000—enough to fill a twenty-foot container! **$12,000**

Then comes the twenty-foot crate. Eagerly Dr. Ray pries it open and finds it stuffed full with everything from stethoscopes to hypodermic needles to latex gloves to all those medications for which he has been so desperate. Almost a million dollars worth of life-saving supplies crammed into that one shipping container. Enough to treat everyone in the waiting room and several thousand more besides. Some of the equipment will be used for years to come.

Suddenly twelve thousand dollars doesn't sound so ridiculously high. Broken down into cost per family, it's just seven dollars. And that sounds downright cheap!

It's all in how you look at it.

LEVERAGING A GOOD DEAL

Almost all the medicines and medical items that go into the shipping crates are donated. Partners International works with agencies such as MAP International, International Aid, Direct Relief and CrossLink International, all of which gather donated supplies from pharmaceutical companies, manufacturers and hospitals in the United States to send them out through organizations that have their own contacts in needy areas— places that can efficiently and effectively get the supplies out to where they will do the most good. (Partners International, for instance, not only works with local churches in the area, but also with Inter-Senegal Mission. World Vision-Senegal assists by enabling the organization to bring the containers into the country more easily.)

When MAP, Direct Relief or the other agencies mentioned here pack a shipping container, they carefully check the expiration date on every medication. Unfortunately not all organizations do this. Some are perfectly happy to pass along the out-of-date meds donated to them for a tax advantage. The scrupulous ones, however, ship only products that can be received, distributed and used before the expiration date.

Direct Relief, a licensed wholesale pharmacy in California, does its best to provide every type of medicine, medical equipment and supplies that a local partner, such as Barthimee Medical Center, requests. It bases its help on need, without regard to politics, religion or the ability to pay. The organization's thousand-plus partners in over seventy countries run the gamut from rural outposts to large hospitals. One thing it does require of a partner is assurance that the materials can be safely delivered—no small task in many areas. In a great illustration of how organizations work together, World Vision-Senegal assists Partners International with these logistics.

These twice-a-year shipping crates are an absolute lifeline for Barthimee Medical Center. Without them, no medicines would be available to restock the ever-dwindling supply on the shelves of the hospital pharmacy. Nor would the mobile clinics have anything to take out to the villages. And key sections of the newly expanded hospital—such as Dr. Ray's surgical unit—would still be unfurnished and without supplies.

Since everything in the crates has been donated, the only cost is a service fee to the collecting organization to help cover its costs and shipping expenses (which don't exactly come cheap, by the way).

Cost of filling and shipping each container? Thousands of dollars.

Value of crate contents? Up to one million dollars.

Physical and spiritual value to communities? Priceless.

When the most recent crate arrived in Dakar, clearing customs in record time, a delighted Dr. Ray zipped this note off to Partners International's headquarters: "Thank you! The arrival of the container was certainly God's perfect timing. For us, it was Christmas in the middle of summer!"

KEY BENEFIT: Accessibility to medications and better medical care helps the entire population of this area of Senegal. Over half the beneficiaries are mothers and babies.

KEY CHALLENGE: Getting a crate of medical supplies loaded and shipped is a costly endeavor, not one that has natural emotional appeal to donors.

6

HOPE IN THE TIME OF AIDS

Fortunate? Kamala? Who was born in a drafty lean-to in a slum in Mumbai, just another one of the hundreds of thousands of the poorest of the poor who are born and live and die on the sidewalks of that teeming city? Kamala, cursed at birth because she dared be born a girl? Who grew up constantly reminded that she was a financial drain on her family and always would be, and the sooner they could get her married off the better, if anyone would have her, that is?

Fortunate is hardly the word most of us would choose for such a one. Not Kamala, who was sold into prostitution at twelve by her family because that way they got money for her and didn't have to shell out for a marriage dowry. Not Kamala, who was forced to join the four thousand other women and girls in the notorious brothels of Bombay's Falkland Road red-light district, 40 percent of whom were already infected with HIV.

CARE FOR HIV/AIDS-AFFECTED MOTHER AND CHILD

HIV is becoming more widespread and feared than leprosy ever was in India. Your gift will help rescue one AIDS-affected mother and her children from the streets of Mumbai (Bombay) and provide a loving home, medicine, vocational training for the mother and schooling for her children for one month. **$320**

Where escape was next to impossible, and even if she managed it, where could she go when she had no home and no family who would accept her? Not Kamala, whose only hope for survival was climbing the rickety staircase again and again to the ramshackle room at the top.

Fortunate?

Tiny Nirmal, Kamala's son, who was born in the brothel? With no chance of a real life because no one wanted anything to do with a brothel kid—except criminals? Even if he should manage to survive there?

Fortunate. Outrageous to use such a word! Then again, as Kamala would be quick to remind us, *fortunate* is a relative term.

AIDS IN INDIA

Because of India's staggeringly huge population, the country's rate of HIV/AIDS strikes us as deceptively low—less than 1 percent. But this figure masks a horrifying problem: one in every eight of the world's HIV-infected people lives in India. Each year the number is growing by half a million. The CIA-affiliated National Intelligence Council projects that by 2010 as many as twenty-five million Indians will be infected with the virus. Already, more HIV-infected people live in India than in any other country of the world.

Unfortunately the bad news doesn't end there. It used to be that AIDS in India was mainly a disease of high-risk people, such as prostitutes and careless truck drivers, and that it was confined to the teeming cities. (Of India's estimated eleven million cases of AIDS, almost a quarter are in Mumbai.) But the National AIDS Commission of India reports that's no longer so. The disease is quickly spreading into the rural areas—which make up 75 percent of India's population—and it's making major advances into the general population.

Pretty grim statistics. Next to hopeless.

Not completely hopeless, however. Not yet.

AN OASIS OF HELP

In 1994, India's Christian leaders looked out at the swarming crowds of destitute and marginalized people in their huge cities, and they wept. They had to do something. What they did was form an organization of refuge that they aptly named Oasis. Then they headed for the slums in search of ways to minister to the discards of society.

Every major Indian city has slums. Mumbai, however, has given the word a horrifying new face—and in the most perplexing way. In a city of 18.5 million people—rife with corruption, crime and harsh inequity—million-dollar apartments overlook the slums where millions struggle simply to survive. Most recently, farm workers, driven from their villages by drought, have swarmed in to join the conglomeration of starvation-level impoverished from many backgrounds and many cultures. Desperation throws these people together and packs them into every possible square foot of space in the illegal slums. With no other place left, the newcomers were forced to settle in areas formerly avoided even by the most desperate—the sewage dumps. There they pieced together lean-tos and makeshift shelters, and they called it home.

Over 80 percent of India's population lives on two dollars or less per day. In the slums, such a sum would seem luxurious indeed. "On average, most make enough to buy one piece of bread for each child per day," said Cherylann, area director for Sisters In Service (SIS), a nonprofit organization that mobilizes and equips advocates to extend God's love to women and children through local partnerships in the most desperate parts of the world.

From its beginning, Oasis emphasized networking with many ministries and agencies for the betterment of the poor and marginalized. In addition to ministries such as SIS and Partners International, the organization works alongside local churches. And it has grown quickly.

Today the many facets of Oasis include a successful daycare center for India's so-called platform children (kids who have been abandoned at

An HIV-positive mother and daughter find a place of help and hope
at Oasis (by Partners International)

railway stations and left to survive any way they can). It also conducts
workshops for people who have never known anything but life on the
street or in the slums, training them in skills that prepare them to lead
productive lives as contributing members of society.

But a major part of the work has been directed toward one of India's
most scorned and neglected segments: prostitutes. Like Kamala, many
of these women were sold to the brothels by their families—some as
young girls and others by their husbands. Others were kidnapped and
sold by traffickers. Many ended up there simply because they saw it as
their only possibility for survival. However she got there, once a woman
is in a brothel, she has no way out. Unless . . .

In a few progressive programs, such as the one offered by Oasis,
workers go into the brothels and actively assist women who want to
leave prostitution. Once out, the women are given a temporary place to
stay. But space is extremely limited in shelters, and the goal is to help

women become self-supporting so they can live independently. So right away, Oasis starts preparing them to earn a living. "Fully three-quarters of the women who move out are able to remain in a stable, healthy environment after two years," one of the Oasis workers told us.

Fortunate . . . for those women healthy enough to take advantage of this program. But what about those who are not? More and more, that's what the Oasis staff members were seeing: sick women. And a great many were rapidly growing worse. At first many tested positive for HIV, but soon an alarming number had full-blown AIDS.

The problem was, Oasis wasn't set up to handle sick women. Certainly not on that scale. Staff members had no idea how to help those infected with HIV/AIDS. The women needed medicine and doctors. What they really needed was to be in the hospital. "We tried to take them, but they were turned away," one worker said, shaking her head sadly. It seems the doctors preferred to reserve hospital beds for people they didn't consider already under a certain death sentence.

As if that wasn't enough of a crisis, many children of the infected mothers also had HIV/AIDS. The virus was passed along to them at birth, before their mothers even knew they were sick. And for the little ones, no medical help was available either.

For the women, who had nothing and never did have anything, the response to this new affliction was resignation. "When I found out I had AIDS, I didn't really care that much," Kamala said. "My life had always been unhappy, and it really didn't matter if I died. Why would I want to live anyway?" But the workers at Oasis cared.

Fortunate.

HOUSE OF WHOLENESS

In 1997, Oasis set up a residential care facility that they aptly called Purnata Bhavan, which is Hindi for House of Wholeness. Strategically located eighty miles outside the streets of Mumbai, the House of Wholeness was established specifically as a place for women and children infected and affected by HIV/AIDS. Hospital doors may have been shut tight, but at the House of Wholeness, the doors were wide open. There the women and their children could find a stable and loving home.

Since the House of Wholeness opened, Oasis has trained many Christian workers to meet the needs of HIV/AIDS sufferers. At the time of this writing, fifty women and children live at the house, where they receive nutritious food, health care and counseling. Because it is run by Christians, the women also have another opportunity. "I learned to do so many things at the House of Wholeness," Kamala said. "And I had a nice place to live. I could help others too. But most important, I came to know God."

The women are required to begin learning a skill that will provide an income to support them and their children. They might choose candle making, for instance, or tailoring or embroidery. Some women learn more than one skill. An organization in Hong Kong has contracted with the women to buy their ornate embroidery work. "They love our work," one woman said. "And we can earn money from them."

Half the money a woman earns goes back to the house to pay for her supplies, but the other half goes into a savings account kept for when she moves out and is ready to live on her own. Getting established is much easier when a woman has not only a marketable skill but also a bit of money saved up.

Because women are working toward self-sufficiency, their training includes going out into the community and lining up orders. "It's hard to ask for jobs," one woman said. "We aren't professionals yet."

It helps that they begin by charging less for their work. As they meet with success, their confidence grows. And the more they do, the more skilled their work becomes. The more skilled their work, the more they can charge.

Few of the women who come to Oasis have had the advantage of schooling, so they also learn to read, write and do simple math. Each one is also expected to help keep the household running by chipping in with the cooking, cleaning and so forth. Each also receives individual guidance and counseling to help her deal with her own particular issues.

Through the training, the women develop such life skills as learning to take responsibility and be accountable for their actions. It's all preparing them for the time when they will move out and take their place as a productive part of the community.

Never before have such learning opportunities been available to these women. Never before have they received such encouragement for their efforts. Most important of all, for the first time in their lives, women once written off as despised outcasts are treated with love, acceptance and respect. They experience the love of Christ firsthand.

On the streets of Mumbai, AIDS-infected women such as Kamala couldn't hope to survive more than a few years. But when they receive nutritious food and medical attention, when they are given what they need to fight infections and other effects of AIDS and when they are given a reason to live, their lives are greatly prolonged. "I can raise Nirmal," Kamala said with a sense of wonder. "He has a mother who is still alive. I can watch my son grow."

How fortunate for both of them.

THE LONG ARM OF AIDS

Puniwati wasn't a prostitute. She was just the extremely young wife of a truck driver who spent far too much time away from home. Puniwati was only fifteen and pregnant with her first child when her mother-in-law took her to a clinic for a routine checkup. No one expected the doctor's diagnosis: HIV-positive.

"I couldn't understand," Puniwati said. "I thought if I was a good wife, I could never get such a disease. And I was a good wife."

Puniwati had contracted the virus from her husband. He died shortly before their daughter, Renu, was born. Blaming Puniwati for their son's death, and not in the least interested in supporting a baby girl who would grow up to require a marriage dowry, Puniwati's parents-in-law threw both of them out of the house and locked the door behind them.

Alone and sick, with a new baby to care for and no way to earn a living, Puniwati was referred to the House of Wholeness.

Very soon baby Renu began to fall ill. At first Puniwati didn't think much about it. Babies were always getting sick, weren't they? But when it happened again and again, the staff insisted on taking Renu for tests. The result was devastating. She too was HIV-positive. "If not for the House of Wholeness," said Puniwati, "well . . ."

SUFFER THE CHILDREN

Not all the children at the House of Wholeness are HIV-infected. Nirmal is not. He's one of the healthy children who live there with infected mothers. But healthy or sick, the children's lives have not been easy. Most have never been to school, which is not surprising, considering the great discrimination children of HIV-infected parents suffer. They are routinely separated from other children, because so many people are afraid children with infected parents will "contaminate" others.

The House of Wholeness is located in a strongly militant Hindu area that has been extremely resistant to the gospel. At first, the local people demanded that children from the House of Wholeness not be allowed in the public school. But the nuns who ran the school stepped forward. "The children can come!" they insisted. "If you are too afraid to allow your children to have contact with them, then it is your children who will have to stay home."

The nuns stood firm. And the House of Wholeness staff worked hard to build good relations with the local schools. Staff also worked with the children, making certain each got the tutoring necessary to get up to speed so they would fit into the classes with other children their age. The approach has been exceedingly successful.

Children from the House of Wholeness have done well academically, and they have stood out athletically. As proof, the house walls are decorated with achievement medals. Recently the top girl student in the school—who was from the House of Wholeness, by the way—was asked to share in the cultural program. Proudly she stood before the other students, the teachers and the parents and sang a medley of Christian songs.

When we visited the House of Wholeness, the children ran up to greet us with giggles and shy smiles. Then they gathered together and sang "God Is So Good" at the top of their lungs.

Fortunate. Instead of begging in squalor, instead of doing their best to dodge those who would harm them, instead of being taunted and chased away from school, those children sang joyfully of a heavenly Father who loves them.

And Hope . . . Still Hope

Hope also comes in many shades. In their time at the House of Wholeness, both Puniwati and Kamala have seen and experienced many painful things. Yet they appreciate the emphasis the House of Wholeness puts on restoring a sense of life and hope for women who have come from backgrounds flooded with loss and hopelessness, who have suffered and suffered some more, who have seen far too much death and despair.

Imagine: What might it be like to believe there was not one worthwhile moment in your life? That you had not one single thing to offer society?

"All we have is our hope in Christ. Without him, there is nothing for us," Kamala said. "Our faith motivates us to work so we can offer people the hope of eternal life." She no longer lives at the House of Wholeness. With the help of the staff, she was able to find a small house that she and her son share with two other women and their children. She makes a living sewing saris and decorating them with intricate embroidery, just as she was taught.

Using the training and the business skills they learned at the House of Wholeness, the four women have developed a self-help group with other HIV-positive women who are also living on their own. Each week, they meet together to help and encourage one another and to save money together. They now have something they never dared believe was possible: a future for which they can plan. "We're all going to die," Kamala said. "We didn't have to learn how to do that. But we did have to learn how to live."

Puniwati, who is on medication and doing well, now works at the House of Wholeness as a counselor and also at the daycare center. She is also always ready to do anything else that needs to be done. Puniwati is known for her radiant love for Christ. "I'm infected with AIDS," she said, "but I'm more infected with the love of Jesus."

Last year, her little daughter, Renu, suddenly grew sicker. "There's no hope for her," the doctors told Puniwati. But Puniwati wouldn't give up. Day and night she stayed by her daughter's bed and prayed for just a little more time with her. Amazingly, against every prediction of the doctors, Renu improved enough to come home from the hospital. "God did answer my prayer," Puniwati said. "He gave us more time together."

Yet Puniwati harbored no false dreams. She had been at the House of Wholeness too long for that, and she was too well acquainted with the advanced stages of AIDS. She had seen far too many women and children die. Even as she prayed, she cradled her daughter in her arms, sang to her and whispered words of peace.

I never got a chance to meet Renu. I only heard her story. And although tears streaked down Puniwati's cheeks as she spoke of the loss of her daughter, I couldn't miss the joy that beamed from deep inside her. Spreading her arms to the children around her, she said, "See? I have many children. God has given them to me. These are his children for me to care for."

Many loving, caring people resist donating for HIV/AIDS causes. This is especially true when organizations focus on women like Kamala who have been involved in prostitution. It's so much easier to lower our eyes and turn toward the sweet innocence of hurting children. Or to reach out to people who are starving or struggling to find clean water for their families to drink, because we know we couldn't live without food or water either. It's easier to empathize with those who have not . . . well . . . you know.

And yet some donors are able to look into the darkest recesses of need and find the grace to help these most rejected of women and children. For that, women like Kamala and Puniwati are fortunate indeed. And not only them. For the House of Wholeness has demonstrated God's love to the entire community. People on all sides couldn't help seeing that women were being restored. That those women who settled among them sewed beautiful clothes and lived well. That their children excelled in school and sang of Christ's love at the cultural program. That the joy of life replaced the gloom of death that had hung so heavily over them. That hope was driving out despair right before their eyes.

The community has witnessed Jesus Christ changing lives. And they are taking note.

"God is good," Puniwati said. "My life is good because of the new life God has given me. And my tears are tears of joy."

KEY BENEFIT: With HIV/AIDS, the most serious health problem in India, and with the hopelessness of affected and infected Indian women and children, offering help and options to these most vulnerable is an absolute necessity.

KEY CHALLENGE: The sheer numbers of HIV/AIDS-infected women is overwhelming, as is the enormity of the need for help. The limited facilities cannot begin to accommodate those in need.

7

A PLACE OF REFUGE

As blowing dust sandpapered the barren landscape, I sat on the ground with three refugee women, all bunched together in the spotty shade of the one tree. Desperate for relief from the searing heat, I first gulped from my water bottle, then dabbed my face with a damp cloth.

"You never get used to it," Lydia told me. "No matter how long you're here, the sun never stops baking the life right out of you." She would know. Fleeing Sudan's endless civil war attacks in the south, Lydia had made her way to the impoverished city of Khartoum so long ago that her memories of home were distant and fuzzy.

Alima sat on my other side. Compared to Lydia, she was a relative newcomer to the city crammed with more than thirteen million people. Just five years earlier she had fled her burning village and, with three young children in tow, had made her way north.

RELIEF ASSISTANCE FOR A REFUGEE FAMILY

Many thousands of Sudanese remain in refugee camps. Your gift will help rebuild hope by providing food and clothing for a family still in a camp or farm tools and seeds for a family returning to the south. **$50**

Faith May, sitting between the other two and across from me, didn't have much to say—only that she had been in this wasteland far too long.

Only that she was counting the days until she could take her children back home.

Lydia, Alima and Faith May are but a tiny sampling of the many thousands of displaced people who have flooded into northern Sudan over the past twenty-plus years. Each one is an individual with a distressingly individual story to tell. Yet in many ways these three women typify the refugees of northern Sudan. Frustrated and discouraged, they speak passionately. Yet their words come with a surprising measure of hope.

"Mostly I think about the children here," said Lydia. "Life is so hard, and they do suffer. It's very discouraging."

"And it's hot!" added Faith May.

"But we won't give up hope, and we won't quit," Alima said. "We can't."

That's what places Sudanese refugees among the most amazing people I've ever met. Driven out of their shattered homes and into hostile areas, they struggle against immense odds, yet they refuse to give up. Knocked down on every side, they continue to get back up and try again.

They don't give up hope and they don't quit. They can't.

SUDANESE CHRISTIANS

The civil war in Sudan has been one of the twentieth century's longest ongoing wars, claiming more than two million lives and displacing more than four million. Over the years, peace talks have come and peace talks have gone. Yet thousands continued to be forced from their homes, leaving everything behind. Some managed to escape to refugee camps in neighboring countries such as Uganda, where they eke out a subsistence-level existence. Many others—including Lydia, Alima and Faith May—were forced up into the arid north, where sprawling displaced-people camps skirt Sudan's capital, Khartoum.

"Crippled people and old people who can hardly walk, they straggle in here all alone," said Faith May. "Sometimes young people come carrying their grandmothers on their backs."

"Those who make it here, we make room for them," said Lydia. "Even though the camps are already too full, we squeeze over and make room."

I asked if many of the people in the camp were Christians. "Oh, yes," Alima said. "Very many. Because the Christians are treated especially badly. That's why they in particular have to run."

For much of the past half-century, Sudanese Christians have suffered persecution. But since Sudan was declared an Islamic Republic in 1983, their suffering has worsened. Operation World reports that in an attempt to eliminate Christianity and its influence, churches have been bombed, hospitals and schools destroyed, and Christian villages laid waste. Pastors and church leaders have been killed and Christians massacred. Refugees, driven into the deserts with no provisions, have been bribed with food to convert to Islam. Become Muslims or starve to death.

According to the government of Sudan, Islam must inspire all of the country's laws, institutions and policies. Banks and businesses are shaped by Islam, as are hospitals and the police force—and, of course, the schools, which are required to teach Islam. If Christian parents can't be forced to convert, then their children will be indoctrinated—early, systematically and thoroughly.

All this presents Christian refugees with truly agonizing decisions. "If you are sick and go to the hospital but don't have money to cover the treatment, they will say there is an office here that has money to help you," said Pastor John, an Africa Inland Church-Sudan leader in Khartoum. "At that office they ask if you are a Christian or a Muslim. If you say you are a Christian, they say they have no money for you. You can imagine the difficult choice of someone who is very sick—will he die or choose the money and Islam? The political situation in the country is designed to make Christians poor so they can be easily exploited or converted."

"We are discouraged, yes. But we know there's a reason for us to be here," Alima said. "We're missionaries—not by choice, but by God's appointment. If it weren't for us, people in the north would never hear about the true God of grace and love. No outsiders can do what we can do here."

What Sudanese believers see is God scattering the Christians of their country the way he scattered the early church. Although it's painful and they suffer terribly, they look on this scattering as an effective method of spreading the message throughout the land. When Christians were forced to run, they simply took their faith along with them.

Wherever they have been dispersed, faithful believers have raised up congregations, even in the most inhospitable of areas. In southern Sudan, the Christian population has increased from 5 percent in 1960 to about 70 percent in 2000. In the Khartoum area, only thirteen churches existed when the first wave of persecution hit. Now there are more than four hundred. And if ever there was a difficult place for Christianity to grow, this is it.

PLIGHT OF THE FAMILIES

From a nearby lean-to, a woman pushed aside the ragged sheet covering the doorway and stared out at us. A little girl peeked out from behind her. Across the yard, a woman swathed in tattered, orange cloth sat on a wooden bench with her somber little son on her lap. When I looked her way, she flashed a huge grin, revealing two missing front teeth. Families. I asked the women around me about their own.

"When the armed rebels came, my husband sent me north with the children," Alima said. "We didn't take anything—just the clothes we were wearing. He said he'd catch up with us in a few days and bring what we needed." But then the police raided the church and dragged Alima's husband off into the night. No one ever saw him again. "Men who were there told me what happened," Alima said, her voice barely more than a whisper. "The police lined up a group of Christians and shot them all in the head. My husband was one of them."

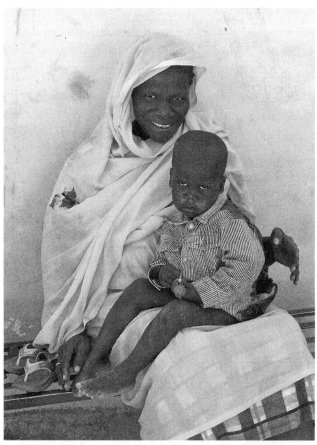

A Sudanese refugee mother and her little son (by Kay Strom)

Alone in Khartoum with three frightened, hungry children, Alima's fit the most common description of a displaced family: two out of three refugee households are run by widows or women who have lost contact with their husbands.

Faith May's husband, a policeman in southern Sudan, was accused of being with the Sudan People's Liberation Army. He was kidnapped and never heard from again. "Everyone assumes he's dead," Faith May said. "They're probably right."

Her family, which is primarily non-Christian, pressed her to obey custom and remarry one of her deceased husband's brothers. But they already had wives, and as a Christian she couldn't do it. So she remains a widow—and the head of her family.

Still, families headed by men are not much better off. Most men can't get work. If they do, it's only low-paying, menial jobs. Before, most were farmers. But in Khartoum, there's no land to farm. And when other jobs become available, Muslims get first choice.

Lydia's husband, George—whom she described as "a fine, fine man"—works at the refugee camp. They had five children, but none survived. Yet Lydia speaks of her family as including four little ones. They are foster children, placed with Lydia and George by the church. "So many children here are alone," Lydia said. "They're sad and hurting, and they have no relatives to take them in. And all the generosity has been stretched out of their neighbors. So the church takes them and finds Christian foster families for them."

Several years ago Alima married Samuel, whose wife was killed in Uganda. Although he works as a carpenter, he cannot earn enough to support their family of ten—Alima's three children and his two surviving sons and three orphaned nieces.

"Two weeks ago my fifteen-year-old nephew showed up in Khartoum," Alima told me. "Somehow he walked all the way from Uganda, through the dangerous passes and past the armed guards, and he managed to find me. His parents—my brother and his wife—were killed, and he wants me to go back with him to get his two little brothers and bring them here. Every day he cries for his brothers and begs me to go get them. But even if I could make that dangerous trip, how can we support three more boys?"

I asked her what she would do. Go, she said. Of course she would go. "This is the price of war."

Orphans. Pieced-together families. Burdens piled onto the backs of the relentlessly overburdened. Such is the situation in Sudan.

"We only survive by the will of God," said Faith May.

Alima nodded. "Though the whole world forgets us, God knows."

Help for Refugees

Perhaps, if the peace agreement holds, Sudan can at long last begin to recover. That's a big *if*. Still, in the camps outside Khartoum, hope grows.

"Most will be going back home," Alima said with a surprising air of assurance.

And while Lydia and Faith May both agreed that's what they wanted, they cautioned that it would be difficult. "We have no money," Lydia pointed out. "The government wants us to stay here in the north and work for them, so they will make it hard for us to leave."

"But we would own land there," Alima argued. "We wouldn't have to pay this high rent. We could work for ourselves and save money and educate our children."

"They want us to stay here," Faith May said, "but they want us here as Muslims, not Christians. That's why we must go back soon. We must take our children home."

Already Samaritan's Purse is helping prepare the way by working with local people in southern Sudan to rebuild churches the government destroyed. Samaritan's Purse provides a resource team, the necessary equipment and the materials—sand and gravel—as well as rice and beans for the workers. The local Christians provide the labor. Together they can have a church rebuilt in just a month or two.

Still, hope doesn't replace reality. Not in the harshness of Sudan. Years of war, destruction and neglect cannot quickly be undone. In many areas, everything must be rebuilt. It will take years—and huge resources. In the meantime, returning refugees will need shelter and food. And clothes and medicines. And mosquito nets, blankets, soap and salt. If they are to begin rebuilding their communities and their livelihoods, they will also need agricultural tools such as hoes, shovels and gloves.

And seeds to plant. All that can be purchased in Sudan or neighboring countries, then delivered to the villages.

All that's needed are donors who share the hope and see the possibilities.

Women's Training Center

Many desperate Sudanese women take advantage of an illegal and dangerous way to earn extra money—brewing beer at home. Although this is an offense to Muslims, whose religion forbids drinking alcohol, there seems to be no shortage of customers.

One day, a woman named Ella was brewing at home when policemen burst through her door and arrested her. When her husband got home, neighbors told him what had happened, but it took him several days to find out where Ella was being held. The penalty for her crime, he was told, was six months in prison plus a hefty fine.

Ella's husband had no money. In that case, he was told, his wife would stay in prison for an entire year. All that time, their children would be left alone to scrounge for food as best they could. In desperation, Ella's husband went door to door, begging and pleading for gifts, for loans, for extra work. Anything.

"We did what we could to help in the name of Christ," Faith May said.

Money was collected and Ella was released. Immediately the Christian women surrounded her with love, modeling the very truths her life had been missing. "We invited her to come to the Women's Training Center," said Alima.

It was out of a desire to enable refugee women to earn money honestly that Alima and Faith May had started the program. The concept was simple: find women who knew how to do something and enlist them to teach others. They started with tailoring. Women learned to make the fabric, to dye it and then to fashion and sew dresses—and even suits for men.

The response was overwhelming. "But we can only take as many women as the center can accommodate," said Alima.

In 2005, the center was able to move into a new building of its own.

"Most women can't even read and write when they first come to us," said Alima. "How can they run a business if they can't count money? Besides reading and writing, we train them to use money and figure profit, and to buy supplies in the market."

"Women just need a boost," said Lydia. "Once they get started, they can bring in a steady income without any more help from us."

NOT ALL SUCCESSES

That's not to say that every business venture has been successful. It's hard to sell one's wares in a place where no one has money. Tailoring is lucrative, but not many of those trained can actually do it because it requires a sewing machine, and few can save enough to pay for one.

Through the generosity of donors, one group of women received thirty cows so they could start a dairy. Wise idea, it seemed. Milk for the children and an income for the women. Until the morning they went outside to tend their cows and found the pen empty. During the night, the animals had all been stolen.

"The women came to us and begged for another chance," said Alima. "They said, 'This time, give us something raiders won't think is so valuable.'" Now those women knit blankets. It's not nearly as profitable an enterprise as raising dairy cows, but in a land of lawlessness and despair, it offers hope.

NEW HOPE

"When you train a woman, you train the whole nation," Alima said, "because it's the women who are raising up the next generation. Children look at their mothers and they are encouraged to do something with their lives. They say, 'Now I see that anything is possible!'"

It's true. Women who once escaped their homeland by running for their lives will return with new skills, empowered to work alongside their husbands. And when they go back, they will leave a changed northern Sudan. No longer can it be said, "There is no Christian witness here."

"Right here, in this desolate camp, the Spirit of God is at work," Faith May said. "There's no more fighting, not even with Muslims. That can only mean Christ is working here. Muslims hear us singing and they see our love and they say, 'What is this? Black people coming together, beating the drum, singing praises?' And then they sneak in and listen to us, and then the Holy Spirit gets their hearts too."

What Christian refugees will leave behind is a legacy of Christ's love in action.

"Every day we meet to pray for Sudan," said Lydia. "We pray that the next president will be a Christian and that the country will be united in the love of Christ. That's what will finally change Sudan."

"One day everyone will raise his hand and praise the Lord," said Faith May. "Not just here in Sudan, but all around the world. We are working toward that day."

As we prepared to leave Sudan, women and children and families gathered around to bid us goodbye. "Don't forget us!" Faith May called out. "Please, don't forget us! You in America, you bring us hope for the future."

"Yes," Pastor John called. "When you pray there, God works here."

KEY BENEFIT: After so many years and so much suffering, thousands of Sudanese refugees are looking forward to returning home. As they rebuild their lives, they will be in a unique position to establish a more stable foundation for the Sudan of tomorrow. This project gives Americans a rare opportunity to get involved in international affairs in a way that can really make a difference.

KEY CHALLENGE: The country, which has declared itself an Islamic republic and in which 65 percent of the population is Muslim, will not easily abide a strong Christian presence.

8

A Blessing Disguised

We hiked up a narrow, winding alleyway squeezed into the shadow between two ancient buildings—four Americans single-file behind Sonia, Marco and Diego. Three little boys halted their ball in mid-kick to stare as we paraded past. Sonia stopped us in front of a dented, white metal door, distinguishable from all the other dented, white metal doors by its generous splash of painted blue dots. We followed up a steep tile staircase, past an open kitchen door. Sonia left her shoes on the landing under the dripping sink, so we did the same. Then we settled in the sitting room on sofas piled high with pillows.

"Doesn't the room look nice?" Diego asked. "They painted it just for today. To honor us." An honor indeed, for we were in the home of an extremely poor family. It was them we had come to meet.

Across the room, three women in headscarves whis-

> **THERAPY FOR A DISABLED CHILD**
>
> In North Africa, disabled people are often looked upon as a curse. Your gift provides one month of physical and occupational therapy for a child in North Africa, while enabling the child and family to hear of God's love and care for them. $31

pered nervously among themselves. They focused their attention on the children on their laps, but now and then one would glance shyly over at us before quickly looking away. Then the tiniest child wriggled off her mother's lap. Curls bouncing and huge, dark eyes shining, she stood unsteadily, then with jerky steps made her way toward our side of the room.

"Meet Yasmeen," Diego said. "This is the beautiful little girl whose parents abandoned everything to bring her hope and give her a chance at life."

Not a curse but a blessing (by Kay Strom)

BABY YASMEEN

Mouloud and Saida had long wanted a baby girl. By the time she was finally born, their two sons were already half-grown. But Yasmeen's was a difficult delivery, and the baby came into the world with barely enough strength to gasp for breath. Neighbors who had come to rejoice shrank back in dismay at the sight of the limp infant who hardly seemed alive. Even the couple's own families turned their backs in rejection.

"Cursed, that's what everyone said," Saida whispered. "There was a curse on us and on our house."

The woman next to Saida grabbed her arm. "Hush, hush!" she warned. But Saida shook herself free.

"What's wrong?" I asked Diego.

The others didn't want Saida to speak aloud of the curse, he explained. Certainly not to us, not to strangers.

In North Africa, to say that a disability is a curse is not just an empty cliché. No, it's a solemn conviction. People believe that surely such an affliction means someone in the family has offended God. Broken his law, most likely. Or perhaps the disability was a protection graciously bestowed on a sinner, a barrier to prevent that child from growing up to do something terrible, such as become an assassin or sink into prostitution. Either way, the best a family can do is humbly accept God's punishment and banish the child to a back room.

"No!" said Saida. "I never did believe my daughter was a curse."

Baby Yasmeen grew older, but it was a long time before she could lift her head. And she never sat up or walked or said a word. Day after day after day she lay on her back on a pallet, alone in a dark room.

"Give up on her," everyone advised. "Face it, you have no daughter."

But Mouloud and Saida refused. And then one day they heard of a place that helped children like Yasmeen. Although it meant turning away from the village where his family had lived forever, leaving all his friends and family, and abandoning his livelihood, Mouloud announced that they would pack up their lives and move to the city so they could get help for their daughter. The two boys were furious. Everything they had ever known was in the village—their friends, their school, their lives. But Mouloud said, "We will go and you will come with us. Wherever you are, you will have a life. We must give your sister a chance at life too."

While Mouloud settled the family's affairs, Saida took Yasmeen and left for the city. Frightened and with little money, she didn't even have a place to live. But to her amazement, another mother she had never met before invited her and her daughter to come and share her house. So for six weeks, that's where they lived. When Mouloud and the boys joined them, the family moved into the only place they could afford—a single room in a stranger's house.

"It was hard for us, because we were all by ourselves," Mouloud said. "We had always had our family and friends around us. For the first time ever, we had no one."

Quickly though, other mothers at the center befriended Saida. From them, she and Mouloud got to know entire families. "Now we know other parents who have the same problems we have," Saida said. "We talk to each other and help each other. We are all a big family."

"And here," said Mouloud, "no one ever tells us our daughter is a curse."

A PLACE FOR HOPE

An evening Bible study at a Muslim home? With songs and prayers and a freeflowing, back-and-forth, sometime raucous discussion? Well, think of it more as a comfortable extended-family dinner party on an outside veranda with the Muslim call to prayer echoing in the background. Think of companionship and laughter and hospitality of Christians and Muslims enjoying one another as friends. Then think of these friends talking openly and honestly about politics and culture and God at work in the hearts of people.

In my quest to talk with the recipients of donor dollars, I found myself in this most unlikely of places. A teacher of Islam passed a platter of meat-filled pastries across the table to me and said, "If Christians and Muslims could talk together—know each other—then there could be peace in the world. It's impossible to have peace through governments, but when people know people, we can have peace."

Certainly right here was a degree of peace in one harsh corner of the world. This diverse group of Muslims and Christians works together in a program for disabled children. Fatima, at whose house we were gathered, is the director of the center where little Yasmeen has been in treatment for cerebral palsy. Almost all Fatima's family is involved in the work on behalf of children with disabilities. The Christians partner with her, helping to make the center financially feasible.

"Two beliefs—Christianity and Islam—brought together by the handicapped," mused the teacher of Islam. "And together we seek the truth of God."

Most countries in North Africa are overwhelmingly Muslim. Since in the Muslim culture to have a disabled child brings shame on the family, how can these Muslims and Christians work together in love on behalf of those with physical and mental challenges? "They must have a special understanding," said Diego. "And they must have special hearts."

A man named Mohammed, who everyone treated with great respect, commented, "Sometimes I feel as if all of us here are one family, that we are a real community, because we communicate in love."

In North Africa, few services exist for people with special needs. Those with disabilities are simply kept out of sight. Or abandoned and left to survive as best they can. But since 1994, workers from Latin America have worked to bring hope and rehabilitation to this neglected population and their families. Active in various regions of North Africa, they have helped close to twenty thousand people.

Latin American Christians. North African Muslims. Donors from the United States. How did such cooperation come about?

"We're not experts in working with handicapped children," Diego readily admitted. "Mainly what we do is mobilize the local population." They find a local organization that is already doing something (such as Fatima's then-fledgling center), and they form a partnership with it (the answer to Fatima's dreams). Then they connect with interested U.S. donors (through Partners International).

The interesting thing is that something *is* already going on in most places—maybe not actually up and running, but at least in the talking stage. So the task is to locate the right people, to find a way to work with them, and, Diego emphasized, to circumvent politics. They also have to deal with cultural divides, dodging the distrust inherent between groups that have always eyed each other with suspicion.

"Most people who come here from across the sea, they don't really care to get to know us," Mohammed said. "If you give us lots of money and then you go away, we have no relationship with you. But that's not how it is with you people. You stay and work beside us."

Not that money isn't needed. Every other week Fatima proclaims, "I have to close this place! There's no money!" But she always comes back. And it's a good thing too.

"Her work has been the door to all the other work for the disabled in this country," said Diego. "It's like a letter of glowing introduction, an endorsement of partnership. If that door were to close, it would do all of us a lot of harm." And so it comes back to the importance of a relationship.

Working with children with disabilities since 1993, Fatima has no lack of little ones for her program, only a shortage of room. Seventy-five children are currently in the program, with another fifty on the waiting list.

FROM THE OTHER SIDE

In Saida and Mouloud's sitting room, I looked across at the mothers holding two wiggly little girls and one dozing boy. All three children attended the center Fatima runs. I listened as the mothers spoke reverently of Fatima and her helpers, as they expressed their appreciation for all that was being done for their children. For the acceptance and love they felt. For the hope they now dared allow to enter their lives.

"But we need to work with the families too," Sonia said. "Even when the children improve, the minds of the extended family members aren't changed. Our work isn't done until the community's perception is changed."

Mouloud spoke up. His wife was working while he stayed at home, Sonia translated for us, because he hadn't been able to find a job in the city. Not much hope either. Not with half the country's population unemployed. "He wants to say 'Thank you,'" Sonia said. "He could never afford to pay for Yasmeen's treatments and medication. He wants you to give his thanks to the person who gives so great a gift for his daughter. And for him."

Later we sat among the pillows in the freshly painted room, the little children cuddled on our laps. The mothers came in bearing platters piled high with couscous, steamed vegetables and chicken. After that they brought bowls of grated carrots and pineapple and a big plate of fresh strawberries. Then the mothers took their children from us and went back out to the kitchen.

"This food is for us," Diego said. "They won't join us. After we've gone, they'll eat what's left." Then he added, "Leave plenty. This meal cost them so much they probably won't eat again for three days."

"And leave some strawberries," Sonia whispered. "They're very expensive, a dish only for honored guests. Our hosts have probably never tasted them. Leave plenty of strawberries."

A WAY IN

Fatima has a dream: in the future, she wants the country to take responsibility for its disabled population, to provide for them in ways that will allow them to live fulfilled lives of dignity and worth. "A most unlikely scenario," almost anyone with experience in the culture would say. And almost anyone would be right. Except for an amazing turn of events.

When I met Kamal, he was zipping around the basketball court so quickly I couldn't get a chance to talk to him or even to take a proper picture. Hard to believe that only five years earlier he was just another beggar on the city streets. Day after day, he dragged himself out to the street corner where he sat all day pleading with passersby for coins. Each evening, he dragged himself back home to his rickety lean-to.

Born without legs, Kamal had been on his own most of his young life. Until one day when two young men approached him on the street corner, one in a wheelchair and one on crutches. They had a proposition for Kamal: come and play basketball, and never again go hungry or sleep in the cold. It sounded crazy to Kamal, but what did he have to lose?

When he first came, Kamal was about fifteen years old—he wasn't sure of his age. He never left. Today he's a forward on one of the country's championship wheelchair basketball teams. He has played in competitions all across North Africa.

That's not all. Through his training, Kamal has become totally self-sufficient. He lives independently and travels back and forth from the gym by wheelchair. "The wheelchair is my shoes," he said as he zipped past me. "If I take care of my wheelchair, I take care of my shoes."

This wheelchair basketball team has been so successful that the organization is actively promoting similar programs in other North African towns. Unfortunately the required equipment is expensive. The players must wait for their specially adapted wheelchairs. As soon as they get them, they can begin developing their own teams.

Do you think wheelchair basketball is just a frivolous pastime? Think again.

Families that used to be too ashamed to let their disabled family members out of the house, now happily bring them to play ball. One program leader, himself disabled, said, "When they see others, they know they aren't the only one. Me too. If I see another handicapped person, it encourages me and makes me feel more like I can do something."

And there's more. Wheelchair basketball may actually be the thing that will make Fatima's dream for North Africa's disabled population a reality. In its few short years, disabled sports in the country went from unknown to top standings in Arab and international competitions. One player by the name of Rabah was personally received at the State House by the country's president. That momentous meeting paved the way for a major change.

"It's like a fairy tale," Diego said. "The president treated Rabah like he was family. The president invited him into the State House and gave him family gifts. Now, because of him, many handicapped people go to the State House and are allowed to be seen by the president. He asks them their problems and he really listens to them."

Rabah, Kamal and other sports stars have sensitized the president to both the plight and the potential contributions of the country's disabled. Now it isn't just the sports people that interest him. He sees many people with disabilities.

A MODEL CENTER

The president isn't the only official to become involved. The first lady's sister has contributed a considerable amount to an affiliated educational center for mentally challenged young people. Students attend classes in beautiful facilities, all financed by the government. This is an especially exciting training center because of its potential as a model for new centers around the country and as a place to train trainers. Already Fatima has looked it over carefully and has learned from what she saw. Already she has made adaptations to her own program. "We don't have their money, and we don't get the support they get," she said. "But we do see the importance of moving forward with the children every way we can."

When Fatima learned that the local primary school had two vacant, junk-filled classrooms on the top floor, she asked for permission to use them for the mentally challenged children. If she cleaned them thoroughly. And disposed of all the junk. And arranged for qualified teachers. And personally took care of all the details.

Because of her vision, her persistence and her family's backbreaking labor, twenty-two children—formerly written off as uneducable—are now in school full time. Most are from extremely poor families or had been abandoned.

Before too many more years, little Yasmeen could well be sitting at one of those desks, reciting her letters and writing her name. Perhaps she will be reading with her friends. And playing on the playground, her curls bouncing and her dark eyes sparkling.

DOOR OF HOPE

We'll call him Samir. Abandoned by a family who couldn't bear to have a mentally disabled son, he survived alone on the streets. Lately he had taken to hanging around the doors of Fatima's center. He was offered food, but he wanted more than that. He wanted a job. So whenever someone came up the dusty road, Samir took it upon himself to pull the metal door open and then to close it after the person had passed through. No one had to open the door because Samir was there. No one entered without a personal greeting or left without being bid *tariq ssalama* (go in peace).

One day, when Samir pushed the door open for Rogelio, who worked with the sports program, Rogelio said, "Samir, you should come with me and try out for our track and field events." To Rogelio's surprise, Samir left the door and came along with him. To his greater surprise, Samir won against every other team member in every jumping event. Not just won, but won easily. Samir was simply the best jumper Rogelio had ever seen.

At Rogelio's encouragement, all week Samir practiced with the team. On Saturday, Rogelio entered him in the national long jump competition. Samir won.

It just so happened that the Pan-African Track and Field competition was to be held the very next week. But Samir had no passport. He didn't even have official identification papers. Marco and others in the office went to work, calling everyone they knew. At the last minute, Samir made it to the game. And he won second place!

Today Samir is a champion of renown whose fame stretches far beyond his own country. He is the perfect example of a young man who benefited from a donor on the other side of the world, one who saw hope and value in the life of a person with disabilities. In return, Samir has done an immeasurable amount to forward the cause of the disabled of North Africa. Yet when I met him, Samir wasn't demonstrating his prowess on the field, nor was he showing off his impressive slate of medals. No, he was opening the door for me at Fatima's center and wishing me *tariq ssalama*. He was back at work.

AROUND THE WORLD

Hope for people with disabilities is by no means limited to North Africa. Lives are being changed around the world.

In Cambodia, in a village of castoff amputees, Samaritan's Purse built a new school and a church. Through the gifts of goats and fishponds, they provided the villagers with the means to help themselves. Today this village of several thousand is completely self-sustaining.

And hope arrived in the little town of Poznan, Poland, although Wheels for the World almost saw their perfectly laid plans unravel right before their eyes. Wheels for the World, an evangelism program of the California-based Joni and Friends International Disability Center, collects thousands of used but serviceable wheelchairs from across the United States through the efforts of more than one thousand Chair Corps volunteers. These wheelchairs are shipped to seventeen prisons that house Wheels for the World restoration shops, where prison inmates volunteer to restore each chair like new. Then teams of specialists raise their own support to travel to less-developed nations where each wheelchair is customized to fit a needy disabled child or adult. During the distribution, local pastors are invited to share the gospel with the wheelchair recipients and their families. To date, Wheels for the World has given away over 35,000 wheelchairs to disabled people in more than eighty countries.

The Wheels team had come to Poland to distribute 225 wheelchairs and Bibles, to train parents of disabled children and to do disability training in village churches. But the day had hardly begun, and already their plans were in shreds.

The distribution area was far too cramped for the crowd that was fast descending on it. Before the team leader could figure out what to do, streams of desperate people and their families poured in through the open doors. Mothers carried their children on their backs, and fathers hauled their disabled children in on blankets. Others with polio or limb amputations hobbled in or were dragged on stretchers or carried in on wooden chairs. Some were dropped off on the curb by taxi drivers and crawled in.

With so many people packing the room so fast, everything and everybody was thrown into confusion. Quickly the leader gathered the team together to calm nerves and to pray. Then they got to work, greeting each family, assessing each need, locating each preassigned wheelchair. As they worked, they shared the good news of Jesus Christ.

Just as things seemed to be coming together, a tired father with his five-year-old son on his back finally reached the head of the line. He had been waiting for hours for a wheelchair for his little boy. But when the wheelchair was brought out, and the man lifted his son in, the wheelchair didn't fit at all.

"I'm so sorry!" the Wheels seating specialist said. "This is the wrong chair." What she didn't say was that only a few chairs were left. All the best were long gone, and certainly any that would fit a five-year-old.

Still the specialist went to the back and dutifully pushed aside several adult wheelchairs. Then . . . yes, there was one child-sized chair, way in the back—the only small one in the entire room. It had been customized with many special features for its original owner, including a blue leather backing with "Jake" stitched across the middle.

When the family saw the wheelchair with all its gizmos, they were taken aback. But the father lifted his son in, and it fit *perfectly!* A circle of curious onlookers had gathered around, captivated by the excited little boy and his perfect wheelchair. "It's like it was made for him!" an interpreter exclaimed.

"By the way," the Wheels specialist asked the boy's mother, "what is your son's name?"

"Jakob," she answered.

God had customized the little wheelchair, not just for one Jake, but for two!

"What a beautiful and powerful ending to a crazy day," said Joni Eareckson Tada, founder of Joni and Friends International Disability Center. "And what a wonderful illustration of Proverbs 19:21—*Many are the plans in a man's heart, but it is the Lord's purpose that prevails.*"

SURPRISED BY BLESSING

The rest of the story is not the same for everyone who receives help. For some, there is a miracle ending. For others, only tiny steps. Yet over and over, workers do see lives transformed. And because of their work among the disabled, they are seeing a growing respect for their own beliefs.

Recently in North Africa police summoned a Costa Rican worker. Fully expecting to be thrown out of the country—if not locked up in prison—he was escorted into the office of the police chief. "Are you working in this area?" the chief asked him.

"Yes, I am," the man answered.

"Are you here because you're helping these people who have disabilities?" Preparing himself for the worst, the man took a deep breath and said he was.

The police chief looked at him and said, "I have called you here because my daughter has been helped by this program, and I want to thank you. Is there anything you need?"

It so happened that the man was having problems with his residency permit. The next day, a policeman knocked at his door. "Welcome to our country, sir," he said as he handed the man a completed permit.

Even we, who had done absolutely nothing to deserve it, experienced that great respect and appreciation as we dined on couscous and strawberries in Saida and Mouloud's newly painted home. "Now we have a daughter where before we had none," Mouloud told us. "And our family is better and stronger because of her. We thank God for Yasmeen. Everyone said she was a curse, but she is our blessing. We thank God for you who help us."

KEY BENEFIT: This gift can lift a disabled child out of a cursed existence in a hidden back room or on the streets, and give that child a chance for a fulfilled and productive life. It is an especially encouraging model to see Christians and Muslims working together toward such an end.

KEY CHALLENGE: In many countries, culture and society don't encourage help for children with disabilities, nor do they view these children as God does—valuable and worthy of respect.

9

SO THAT ALL MAY HEAR

We filled every seat in the large auditorium. On my left was an Indian man from the Dalit—untouchable—caste. His skin was so dark I thought at first he was from Africa. On the other side, next to my husband, was a woman with high cheekbones and distinctly Asian features from Manipur, the northeast Indian state that juts up against Myanmar (Burma). In front of us were Indians from Sri Lanka and South Africa. People had also come from Singapore, Indonesia and Nepal, from Canada and the United States.

"Call out your first language, and I'll list it on the board," said Ramadu from the platform in front. By the time he was finished, he had listed forty-one different languages. Then all together we sang "God Is So Good," each of us in our own language.

"This is how it will be in heaven," Ramadu told us. "Around God's throne, gathered from all nations, we will be praising God together!" This was so appropriate in India, the ancient melting pot of races and cultures. So

TRAINING FOR A CHURCH PLANTER

Training of a church planter is a key element for the church to grow among unreached people groups. Your gift provides one church planter with special training in how to communicate the gospel in another culture. . . . . **$70** appropriate in a land where 1,652 distinct languages are spoken.

Amazingly, India isn't that large a country. It's only about one-third the size of the United States. Yet while it has just one-fortieth of the world's landmass, it is home to one-sixth of its population—a staggering 1.1 billion people.

India is also an extremely complex country, defined by numerous caste divisions that have traditionally resulted in crushing oppression and exploitation for those unfortunate enough to be at the bottom of the pile. This is where nearly one-third of the population finds itself. This is the Dalit caste. For many centuries heaped with the indignities of untouchability, still today they often suffer cruel social discrimination and searing poverty. Furthermore the plight of women has traditionally been tragic. Oppression, mistreatment and disdain—still prevalent in many areas—plunge them into a sense of worthlessness that is difficult to overcome. In an irony that increases with India's struggle to be recognized as a global powerhouse, some of the world's richest people live in India but so do teeming masses of its most destitute.

Christianity is nothing new in India. The apostle Thomas is believed to have brought the gospel of Jesus Christ to the country back in the first century—and was promptly speared to death by an angry Brahmin priest. Although there has been a Christian presence there for two thousand years, only 2.5 percent of Indians are Christians. But the most surprising fact of all is that four thousand people groups in that country have yet to hear the gospel even once.

Joshua Vision India (JVI), established and run by Indians, is determined to see that all of India's diverse peoples will have the chance to hear the good news of Jesus Christ. Their approach is to train master trainers, each of whom will choose one unreached people group, then develop a unique, culturally appropriate strategy for approaching that area. With their master plans in hand, they train indigenous grassroots pastors (called harvesters), who plant churches, preach the gospel and disciple new believers among their own people.

In October 2005, the master trainers were invited to come from the distant corners of India and beyond, to gather for five days at the place of their training. Together they could discuss ideas, share strategies and lay out plans for the future. They could rejoice over their successes, and they could also share their difficulties and disappointments. All the things they couldn't talk over with anyone else they could say there. They could learn from one other and also through the seminars and workshops. And as the group raised its collective voice in prayer and praise, each individual could gain strength and encouragement from being a part of the large, united body.

Two hundred people made the trek back "home." What a varied and exciting bunch they were: an academically minded Gypsy, a former Islamic militant scarred by bullets and fire, a beautiful sophisticate from the exalted Brahmin caste, a striking Nepalese gentleman dressed in national garb, a young Asian woman who had cast her lot with the most primitive of tribesfolk, a dozen women who had never before seen a building or a motor vehicle. And many, many more. Some master trainers brought harvesters along with them to receive extra training through such seminars as Bible study skills, witnessing and kingdom principles.

"So many Christians!" gasped one woman as she gazed in awe over the packed assembly room. "I didn't know there were so many of us!"

Ah, but there are. Let me introduce you to a few and show you yet another example of your donor dollars at work.

RAMADU

Banjaras, that's what they are called. Or Gypsies. Or sometimes just filthy bandits. Actually these tribespeople call themselves Ghor, and forty million of them live in India. They are the root of all the world's Gypsies. Mostly they keep to themselves, but if you are fortunate enough to spend time in a Banjara village, you will never forget it: Men beating drums, women dancing furiously in a circle, their brightly colored costumes flashing with mirrors and coins stitched in.

"I grew up worshiping idols and sacrificing goats," said Ramadu. "My family practiced witchcraft. We lived in constant fear, and superstitions controlled our lives. That's the way of our people."

Only a fraction of one percent of India's Banjaras have ever heard the name of Jesus. Yet one day some Christians passed by a Banjara village and gave Ramadu's father a tract to read. This was amazing, actually. Most people cut the place a wide berth, because the villagers were known as rat catchers. It's doubly amazing because only about 15 percent of the tribespeople can read. But Ramadu's father did read the tract, and he was astounded to learn that this God-man named Jesus could forgive sins. Once and for all. Done and done. Ramadu's father knew plenty about asking forgiveness. He appealed to the idols and sacrificed goats in an effort to appease them. Again and again and again. But once and for all? Imagine!

Ramadu was five years old when his father did the unthinkable. He became a follower of Jesus Christ. When others in the village heard about it, they threw his entire family out of the village. Then they seized his land and his animals, then burned his hut and everything in it. Even though Ramadu's grandfather was head of the village, he turned his back and refused to intervene. In a final stroke of rejection, the villagers banded together and denied the family any means of support.

Outside the village, Ramadu huddled against his father. His mother and brothers and sisters gathered around. They were all alone in the desert.

A major festival was just beginning, so the village sacrificed its best goat. All the villagers sat down to eat the meat and to participate in the fellowship of the god, asking for good crops, health and success. The fragrance of roasting meat drifted outside the village gates and over to the hungry family.

"The scraps they offer to the idol will be left," Ramadu's older brother said excitedly. "After everyone goes to bed, we can sneak in and get them."

"No," said Ramadu's father. "We will not scrounge for scraps from the idol. God will take care of us."

The family, persecuted and destitute, did their best to scratch out a living on a tiny piece of land outside the village gates. Never once did Ramadu's father complain. But neither did he believe God wanted the only Christian family in the area to die. So he made a painful decision: he sent his four boys to an orphanage where they would have something to eat, where they would get an education and a chance at life.

Ramadu was the first person in his family to earn a college degree. He vowed it would not be wasted. His enthusiasm and commitment were so great that he was recommended for training at JVI's master trainer program. Except for one small thing: there was no money to send him.

Like Ramadu, all master trainer candidates must be referred by a church or mission organization. While many groups have enthusiastically committed to sending their best workers for the one-year training, the majority simply are not able to afford the cost. This is where donors come in. Simply put, donors make the training possible. Just in time, a gift arrived for Ramadu.

In addition to emphasizing courses relating to the gospel, the program's curriculum teaches technology for the holistic development of the poor and oppressed. Master trainers also become proficient in a specific microenterprise project they can use to support themselves in their new community. And they can teach that enterprise to the poorest people to help them toward self-sufficiency.

For his specific area, Ramadu chose the Banjaras. In fact, he moved back into his father's old village to live among the people who had so persecuted his family and left them to die in the desert. Today half the people in Ramadu's village are Christians. Every Sunday the new church is filled with people praising and worshiping God.

Why the transformation? I wanted to know. "Because Christians were not ruled by fear. They reached out in love and forgiveness to meet the people's greatest needs," Ramadu answered. "When the villagers saw that, they wanted to know what kind of God we followed."

For the first time, Banjara boys were offered a chance for an education. For the first time, magic charms were set aside and children were given health care. When Ramadu and his father came back and lived in the village, their crops grew and prospered. Immediately they shared their bounty with the villagers, then they offered to teach them a better way to grow food. Ramadu gave the villagers cows to raise, which the people immediately decided beat catching rats by a long shot.

And when Ramadu sang songs and told stories of Jesus, people gathered to listen.

From his own village, Ramadu goes out to other Banjara villages with his message. Many times, he will say to someone, "I want to talk to you about Jesus. Do you know who he is?" The answer: "No. That man doesn't live in this town."

"They have never before heard the name of Jesus," Ramadu said. "It's my privilege to tell them for the very first time."

"What a perfect ending to your story!" I told Ramadu.

"Almost perfect," he answered. "My grandfather died last year. He never did accept Jesus."

ALI

Despite an 80-percent Hindu population, India also has a strong Muslim minority (13 percent). In some places, such as the disputed Kashmir area between India and Pakistan where Ali grew up, Muslims are the majority.

From the time Ali was tiny, his Islamic fundamentalist father saw to it that his son diligently studied the Qur'an and Muslim law. To his great pride, Ali was a star student. As Ali grew older, he longed to go to an Arab country where he could learn more about his religion in a purer atmosphere. The closest he got was Pakistan, and he came back burning with passion. In fact, he rained down such persecution on a neighboring Christian family that they fled for their lives. Basking in the glory of that success, Ali followed his father and became a policeman, a position that provided ample opportunity to hunt down and torment anyone he even suspected of being a Christian.

Then one night Ali had a dream. Jesus Christ came to him bearing a cross over his shoulder. Jesus looked at Ali and said, "I suffered for you. Now you take this cross and carry it." Ali jerked awake in a cold sweat. Yes, the person in his dream was Jesus the Christ. There was no question about it. He recognized him from the Qur'an.

Although Ali managed to push the dream aside and go on with his life, over the next several years it came back to him again and again. Each time, he awoke more troubled than before.

Finally Ali could stand it no longer. He sought out a Christian pastor, though he was certain the man would slam the door in fear and bolt it. Instead the pastor welcomed him and listened to his entire story. Then he gave Ali some books to read. Ali started with the Bible. That very night he fell to his knees and accepted Jesus Christ as his Lord and Savior.

So excited was Ali about finding the true Messiah whom he had long seen shadowed in the Qur'an that he ran home rejoicing. "I've found the truth!" he cried to his family. But instead of rejoicing with him, his father pulled out his gun, aimed it at his son's heart and pulled the trigger. At the last moment, Ali ducked, and the bullet lodged in his arm.

Horrified and confused, Ali ran from his father's house and walked thirteen miles to the only person he could trust—the pastor. The pastor called a Christian doctor who was with the Indian army, and he removed the bullet.

As soon as Ali could get up, he walked back to his father's house. Surely it had been a misunderstanding. Surely, once his father heard what the Bible said about Jesus . . .

Ali didn't make it home. His furious father and uncles met him on the road, doused him with gasoline and set him on fire. Though he cannot explain it as anything but miraculous, once again his life was spared. "Right then, I decided I would spend my life serving Jesus Christ," Ali told me.

He went to Bible college, then was sent to the master trainers course. The group on which he chose to concentrate was the Muslims of Kashmir. He could not have made a more difficult—or dangerous—choice.

He has survived stonings. Once, while he was translating a sermon in Kashmir, in a totally Muslim area, one man after another picked up rocks and started throwing them at him. As the rocks smashed him in the head, the face, the stomach, Ali cried out to the police standing all around and begged for help. They merely watched, laughing. As Ali fell to his knees, then slumped to the ground, his wife stepped between him and his tormenters. Figuring he must already be dead, they shrugged and drifted away. Ali survived.

He has lived through bombing attempts. Once, while traveling by train, Ali heard a strange noise and went to another car to investigate. Suddenly the compartment in which he had been riding exploded. The bomb was meant for him, but Ali walked off the train uninjured. Another time, a man rode up and parked his motorcycle on the street corner next to where Ali and a friend stood talking, then walked away. Ali's friend said he could do with a cup of tea, so the two went into a nearby café. Minutes later, the motorbike exploded.

Muslim leaders have put a high price—a fatwa—on Ali's head. While Ali was holding a seminar for Muslims interested in knowing more about Christianity, two young militants intent on killing him and collecting the reward made their way inside. But someone caught wind of the plot and whispered a warning to Ali. He quickly escaped to his hotel and up to his room, but the militants were right behind him. It so happened that the hotel was hosting a large function for a powerful militant Hindu group that embraced the *Hindutva* ideology that teaches "India is Hindu only." They hated Christians, but they hated Muslims just as much. The Hindus wanted them all out of India. So when the Muslim men came running up yelling after Ali, the Hindus rushed over and, with guns drawn, forced them away from the hotel.

Just imagine! A Christian evangelist saved from militant Muslims by militant Hindus! The Lord does indeed work in mysterious ways.

"But, with a price on your head, shouldn't you be more careful?" I had to ask Ali. "Why preach to such big crowds? Why not just teach in houses? in secret places? Why not let other people who don't have so much to lose do the public preaching?"

"No one can take my life from me," he said. "I will not die one day, not one hour before my appointed time. And when it is the appointed time for me to be with God, nothing or no one can keep me here on earth."

PREMLATA

India isn't like Western countries. Male preachers have little contact with women. It isn't considered appropriate. Which is why JVI developed a specific arm of the master trainer program for women. Called Indian Women in Lord's Labor (IWILL), it allows women to become master trainers who go out and work with other women. They too can train harvesters to assist them, and they can also help plant churches.

Women come for training from all over India: from the congested cities to the deserts of Rajasthan, from the foothills of the Himalayas to the extreme south, where homes were washed away by the great tsunami. Although women from all social strata are welcome at IWILL, the vast majority are poor and from the Dalit caste.

Premlata is a striking exception. Light skinned, with cultured manners and an elegant style, she dressed in classy clothes of silk bedecked with intricate stitching and beading. It wasn't difficult to identify her as a revered and privileged Brahmin, a member of India's highest caste.

From a wealthy and highly respected Delhi family, it was Premlata's grandfather who first converted to Christianity from Hinduism. Immediately his entire family rejected him. Overnight he went from great wealth and privilege to outcast. In the eyes of his family, he was no better than a despised untouchable. Although he willingly gave up the many advantages that came with his high caste, in time he did inherit a portion of the family money.

A crucial part of a donor's train-a-church-planter gift goes toward providing the trainer with seed money. This allows workers to develop the microenterprises that enable them to be self-supporting and to give an economic boost to the poverty-stricken of their areas. Donor money is only an initial investment to help trainers launch their income-generating projects, by the way. And it only partially funds it. But the money does help pay for basic materials such as candle and soap molds (in many places, electricity is scarce and undependable, and everywhere contaminated water is a problem) and for whatever is needed for a worker's budding enterprise (a sewing machine, for instance, or electronic repair equipment or farm animals). When workers make enough of a profit from their enterprises, they repay the seed money fund so that it will be available for the next person. People are lined up waiting for loans, but so many are in need that it takes time.

So imagine the gasps that went around the room when Premlata showed up the very first day carrying elaborate candle and soap molds. They were of much higher quality than any the other women had ever seen. "My father bought them for me," Premlata explained a bit apologetically.

As children of God, the women knew they were all one family, and they realized they all came from different areas and from different cultures within India. Still Premlata stood out as someone different from everyone else. And everyone else treated her as someone different. With one another, they laughed and joked and cried and groused. With Prem-

lata, they all sat up straight and behaved themselves and spoke with reverence. At mealtime, they stood aside and insisted she go to the head of
the line. In any discussion with Premlata in attendance, all the women
nodded and bowed their heads. They let her talk, and no one ever dis-
agreed with anything she said.

It will be different in the country, Premlata told herself.

It was different. It was worse. The area Premlata chose as her focus
was extremely poor. The men and older boys had all left the village in
search of jobs in the city, so the population was almost all women and
children. Not one of them could read or write. No school existed in
walking distance. But what most appalled Premlata was the plight of the
widows in the village. With no one to send money back to them, they
literally sat in their huts and starved to death. When Premlata wrote her
strategy for the area, it contained two main elements: start a school for
the children and begin a home for the care of widows. Both would provide her with wonderful opportunities to teach the love of God through
Jesus Christ. Out of that, she prayed, a church would be born.

But from her very first day in the village, Premlata had problems. She
tried desperately to start friendships, but everyone kept their heads
bowed and refused to look the high-caste lady in the face. They stole
glances at her fine clothes, but when a tiny girl dared to walk up and
touch her, the women rushed forward with a collective gasp and yanked
her away. Premlata made candles to light up the village at night, and the
women bowed before her in reverence.

When she went to the village well for a drink, the women rushed forward to grab the cup from her hands. "Why?" Premlata begged. "Why
will you not let me drink water?"

Bowing low the bravest woman replied, "Not from our cups,
madam. Your lips must never touch where our lips have touched. You
are far too great."

Right then, standing beside the village well, Premlata made a decision. "I would get rid of my clothes. There is nothing sinful in them, but why do I need them? It's not proper dress in this poor village. It's a prideful stumbling block that makes it hard for the women to accept me. From now on, I will wear only simple cotton saris."

Reaching her hand out to the women, Premlata said, "We are all one in Christ, my sisters. I would consider it an honor to share your cup."

Before the week was out, four families asked how they might also know and follow Christ.

YESHE

Although the great majority of master trainers work with people groups inside India, some go outside the country's borders to places such as Sri Lanka, Bhutan and Myanmar.

And Nepal.

Ringed by the towering snow-capped Himalayan Mountains, until recently Nepal was the world's only Hindu kingdom. It is one of the poorest and least developed countries in the world. And only a tiny 0.3 percent of its population is Christian.

Even so, Yeshe had heard about Jesus Christ ever since he was a young boy. Every time his uncle came to visit, in fact. Despite Yeshe's father's insistence that his family was not interested, despite threats from village officials, Yeshe's uncle kept right on until his Christian talk got him banished from the area.

But when Yeshe's younger brother died tragically as local healers stood by unable to offer any help, teenage Yeshe reconsidered all he had heard over the years from his uncle. And he decided to follow Jesus Christ. He has never regretted his decision.

After he finished school, Yeshe traveled from Nepal to central India to train as a master trainer at JVI. The unreached area in his heart was his own country. One year later, he returned home to assume leadership of the ministry of the Good Friends of Nepal (GFN).

It was the local religious leaders' helplessness to save his brother's life that had awakened Yeshe to the power of God. And it was God's hand at work when the small group of believers prayed for the sick that allowed them to talk to others about the one who not only heals the body but also forgives sins and saves souls. Yeshe started meeting with the group of believers for fellowship and prayer.

At one point the twelve-year-old daughter of the village witch doctor and her little brother began to creep in to those meetings and listen at the back. They had been doing this for some time when the little boy suddenly fell desperately ill and lost consciousness. His witch doctor father, doing his best to heal the boy, called on every one of his spirit powers. He even made an animal sacrifice. But the boy didn't regain consciousness.

That's when the girl fell to her knees and cried out to God to help her brother. Before her father could punish her for this sacrilege, the boy sat up and looked around. His fever was gone. He was healed.

No longer do the children sneak in and sit in the back of the believers' meetings. No, the witch doctor openly sends them to the church. Although he hasn't yet decided to follow Christ himself, he does eagerly listen to the gospel message.

One of Yeshe's concerns for his country is the lack of education. Half of Nepal's population is illiterate. Although Christians long to read the Bible, most cannot. With the help of Partners International, GFN conducts informal education programs that teach reading and writing. This is not only changing lives, it is also changing society and Nepal's future.

For the vast majority of Nepal's 130,000 orphans, however, there's little reason to plan on a future. Yeshe is determined to change that. An orphanage is another part of his strategic plan.

With Nepal locked in an endless struggle between the government and the Maoists, far too many innocent people have died, especially women and children. And the killing continues. It's especially dangerous for Christians, because both sides are against them. When a Christian worker had the misfortune to be kidnapped by the Maoists and held for ransom, he was finally released only to be badly beaten by the army, who accused him of hiding and feeding the Maoists.

To speak for Christ in Nepal is to attract persecution. No one knows that as well as Yeshe. And yet he's too busy helping his people and training up harvesters to plant churches to let it worry him.

MOALA

At the first rays of sunlight, Moala adjusted the full pack on her back and set off hiking over the mountains. Down deep river valleys she went, and across turbulent streams. Reaching the village she had targeted for her strategic plan was no easy matter. The sun was dipping low when she arrived, yet she shook off her weariness and headed for the fields to work alongside the village women. When one invited her to eat with her family, Moala gratefully accepted, then did her best to ignore the hands covered with dirt and muck as they dropped food into an unwashed pot. As darkness fell, the family asked Moala to spend the night with them in their one-room hut. Edging past goats that had already settled down to sleep, she pushed aside a rooting pig and squeezed in among the children. It was a long, long night.

As Moala lived and worked among the villagers, they began to see her less as an outsider and more as a friend. She was even learning their unwritten language. The women loved her songs, and they sang along with her. She told them stories of Jesus, and the women responded with open hearts.

Living among sun- and moon-worshipers whose lives haven't changed for centuries, sleeping bunched together with children and adults, and pigs, goats and chickens—what a change for a girl who had grown up in a Christian family in the modern Indian state of Nagaland! The youngest of ten children, Moala was dedicated to the Lord's work at birth by her mother. But her mother died in an automobile accident before she was able to see the answer to her prayers.

Actually Moala never planned to go to the master trainer course at all. She was the last-minute substitute for a friend who had to cancel. But as soon as she arrived at the training compound, she knew she was in the right place. And very soon she knew what her focus area would be—the forgotten state of Arunachal Pradesh.

In the far northeast corner of India, many hundreds of villages are tucked into the isolated edge of the Eastern Himalayas. Remote and forgotten by time and the world, they have no schools, no electricity, no running water, no telephones, no access to medical care, no knowledge of basic hygiene, no form of transportation other than feet.

"The people have no food and few clothes," Moala told Cherylann, area director for Sisters In Service (SIS), an organization that partners with her. "Some of them have nothing to eat except wild yams. Not even rice. And for clothes, they just have a thin piece of cloth to wrap around themselves."

Moala was not prepared for what she found in the mountain villages: women who had been married off as young as ten and had borne as many as seventeen children (although seldom did more than two or three survive); hungry families with malnourished children; people with not enough clothing to protect them from the freezing winter cold; mothers who came in from the fields and pushed the pigs away from the cooking utensils to prepare dinner; a short life span and an especially high mortality rate among babies and children.

As she lived among the people, Moala watched and waited for a chance to teach and to train. In the meantime, she accepted offerings of food from the people's meager stores, despite the unsanitary conditions in which they were prepared. "If I don't accept it, it's an insult," Moala said. "So I eat. Whatever is offered, I pray for protection and I eat."

On her fourteen-plus-hour hikes to the villages, Moala can manage to carry only one backpack. As she set off that first winter, she shivered at the thought of freezing through bitterly cold nights with only the one blanket she could squeeze in. As usual, her pack was filled with clothing she'd collected for the children to keep them from freezing. Turns out, the nights were no problem. Lying in the center of the room with all the others in the family snuggled in—and all the animals too—"there was plenty of warmth!" Moala said, laughing.

Moala's district in Arunachal Pradesh has 392 villages scattered throughout the mountains. Only sixteen have churches. Fifteen other districts are similarly filled with villages. Moala is free to go to any of the villages that have churches, but she's not accepted in the others. Even if she were to go, she would have no place to sleep or eat. Her only way to access them is to go with friends and visit one of their relatives. A friend of a relative is always welcomed.

"I say I'm from Nagaland, but that I like the people in that village," Moala said. "I always start with friendship." Moala and her new contacts sit and talk. Then she plays the guitar and teaches them songs. Everyone loves music. They also love hearing stories from the Bible. When it seems right, she asks, "Do you mind if I pray?"

The answer is always, "No, we don't mind."

Many village women tell Moala, "I want to be a Christian—if my husband will let me."

Often when she arrives at a village, weary from her daylong hike, Moala finds the villagers assembled and eagerly waiting for her to start singing and telling stories. So she shakes off her weariness, and for two or three hours straight, she sings songs of praise to God and tells stories from the Bible. When she finally finishes, all she can think of is a warm bowl of soup and a spot on the floor where she can curl up under her blanket.

But no. These villagers—people who for more generations than anyone can count have worshiped Donyi-Polo, god of the moon and stars, people who don't feel dressed unless they have their huge knives at their waists, who think nothing of using those knives against their neighbors—these people clap and cry, "Again! Again! Start the songs and stories over again!" And she does. Even if the telling takes all night.

One of Moala's goals is to organize the village women into self-help groups, which will enable them to become self-sufficient. It will also teach them something else. "If I go to Nagaland, I'm sad because I'm not here with you," Moala tells the women. "I love you and I want us to help each other." Help each other? What a unique idea!

"Right now, you're all alone. But if you form a group, you won't be alone any longer. When you are well or sick, you will no longer be completely on your own." Never before had the women considered such a thing. Help another woman? And someone might help you?

Community is a totally new concept for them. From the age of five, children are left at home alone to care for the younger ones in the family. By the age of eight, they're out in the fields working alongside their parents. What the women do know is loneliness, despair and hopelessness.

A new idea . . . and yet the women are receptive to it. When they actually experience friendship, they truly do appreciate it.

In her first six months at the village, Moala was able to equip and encourage fourteen harvesters from among the women. All of them now lead self-help groups—some three or four. In all, 172 women attend groups in the area, and Moala is in the process of expanding the program to include still more.

"The problem is, it's really difficult to take these women to southern India for harvester training," Moala said. "It's so expensive, and everyone here is very poor. We have no transportation out of our area. We need a training institute up here!"

Despite the regular help she receives from SIS donors and others, Moala is often short of funds. For one thing, the village is so crushingly poor that she ends up digging into her own pockets to help the people with basics such as food and clothes. Like all trainers, she selected a microenterprise to assist with her support and to help the people toward self-sufficiency. Yet this foundation stone of the master trainer program is especially difficult for her. Even though she chose what looked to be the easiest and most basic product to make and sell—candles—she soon found that the supplies weren't available in the area. Telephones are unknown, so they couldn't be ordered either. Anyway, the closest mail service is hours away and exceedingly slow. So every three months, Moala treks to southern India for supplies, then she carries everything—the wax and the heavy metal candle molds—to the village on her back.

Candle making is an excellent skill, and it fills a real need in the villages. But the greatest microenterprise problem is that no one has money to buy anything. How can anyone have a business when there is absolutely no market? Only one answer: redefine microenterprise to fit the context of the culture.

"Village people gather their food and carry it home on their heads," Moala said. "It's hard, and it's time consuming. I'm thinking about opening a little grocery store where people can bring things to barter. They can 'buy' everything they need from each other."

When Moala came to the gathering, she didn't come alone. Twelve wide-eyed tribeswomen harvesters accompanied her. Each one had to walk from her own village, leaving early enough to meet Moala in her village at dawn. Some walked for an hour or two, others for an entire day. From Moala's village, they rode in two taxis for more than a day to get to the state capital. Not one of the women had ever seen a motor vehicle before, let alone ridden in one. Nor had any of them ever seen a building larger than a hut. It was a wondrous—and terrifying—experience. In the capital city, they boarded a bus and rode for three days to get to southern India. What an amazing feat for women who never leave home except to trudge to work in the fields!

"Living in our village is like living in darkness," one tribeswoman said

Worshiping and studying at the gathering (by Dan Kline)

as she looked around her in wonder. "Now for the first time I see light."

"We don't have a Bible, and we don't know how to read," said another. "But we have learned to pray for each other in our group."

Moala looked at the women gathered around her, and she beamed with pride. "I love the people," she said. "I love them very much." She didn't have to tell us. Love was written in her voice. Even more, it shined through her actions.

As the gathering concluded, people were acknowledged and certificates awarded. Then the twelve tribeswomen from remote mountain villages on the edge of the Eastern Himalayas—villages forgotten by time and the world—walked proudly to the platform to receive their certificates. "For successfully completing a specially crafted course for nonliterate church planters," Mary Vijayam, head of IWILL, announced. They could neither read nor write, but they had met all the requirements to become certified harvesters. In the audience, we rose as one and gave the women a standing ovation.

"We are sorry we did not know about this way of life earlier," said one woman with Moala translating. "Our lives would have been so much different if we had known before what we know today."

I pulled out my wallet. I couldn't wait to be a donor. This master trainer and her harvesters were my kind of people.

KEY BENEFIT: The gift of well-trained, culturally sensitive church planters, uniquely able to communicate the gospel to people who have never had the opportunity to hear the name of Jesus, is a gift for eternity.

KEY CHALLENGE: Reaching the most unreached people on earth often seems too hopeless a task to even consider. Yet qualified and willing workers are ready, and training is available. The great need is money.

WHEN DISASTER STRIKES

Taking into consideration all the recent floods and famines and hurricanes and wars and earthquakes, what single event best illustrates donor dollars at work in disaster relief? Not an easy choice, to be sure. So let's just jump back to where we started—that catastrophic year of 2005. Well, actually, let's go back a few days before that, to one of the most deadly natural disasters in recorded history.

Just before eight o'clock on the morning after Christmas 2004, one of the strongest earthquakes ever recorded ripped open the ocean floor off the northern tip of Indonesia and sent waves as high as thirty feet thundering onto the shores of Indonesia, Sri Lanka, India and Thailand. When the water finally receded, coastal communities lay in ruins. Some were completely gone, washed off the face of the earth.

Hardest hit by the tsunami was Indonesia. Some estimate the death toll there as high as 220,000—close to a quarter of a million people in that one country alone.

DISASTER AID

Partners International has long-standing relationships with extraordinary indigenous ministries. These relationships allowed our partners to provide aid and hope to those struck by the Indian Ocean tsunami just forty-eight hours after it hit. Check out ways you can help those still affected. Medicine for survivors in Indonesia. . . . **$8**

Appalling. But that's not all. An incalculable number of other people were injured, lost their homes and everything they owned, lost their livelihoods, suffered psychological trauma from which some will never recover.

Throughout this book, we have seen many exciting donor possibilities. Investments that can change lives and communities, both in this life and the next. Various avenues for transformation, for raising hope out of despair. Yet the fact is that many people automatically equate charitable giving with helping out during times of disaster. It's the catastrophes, it seems, that tear at our hearts and compel us to action. This is, to a degree, as it should be.

Certain organizations, such as the Red Cross and Direct Relief International, are basically relief organizations. For others, relief is right at the top of what they do. After the tsunami, for example, Christian Aid rescue teams were immediately on the scene, pulling people out of the water. And within hours, World Vision began its relief efforts by setting up health clinics and making fortified porridge available to hungry babies. Within the first week, a helicopter belonging to and operated by Samaritan's Purse touched down in areas otherwise inaccessible, bringing basic necessities such as food, clothes, shelter, blankets, and bundles containing stoves, pots and pans. Where government groups were throwing together inadequate barracks to serve as temporary housing, Samaritan's Purse stepped in and quickly constructed permanent housing that immediately became the model for further construction projects.

Other groups, while not essentially relief organizations, are also able to play an important part in times of disaster because of the long-term relationships they already have in the affected areas. Partners International is a good example. Because it partners with capable local Christians in so many areas of the world, it is able to respond to tragedies quickly and effectively. When record rainfalls left two-thirds of Bangladesh under water, for instance, Partners International immediately contacted its partners in the affected area and asked what was needed. A specific list arrived by return e-mail: rice, lentils, salt and cooking oil for four thousand families. Immediately Partners International shot out an alert to its donors, and those desperately needed essentials were provided. The cost was just fourteen dollars per family.

Whatever the thrust of an individual organization, disaster relief is best accomplished when groups come together, each bringing its strengths and assets to the combined effort—secular and Christian, large and small, Western-operated and indigenous-based.

Global Missions International (GMI), the mission arm of Papua, New Guinea, churches, is a good example. After the tsunami disaster, people from GMI who already lived in Indonesia rushed to Banda Aceh and set to work alongside men and women from Samaritan's Purse and other Western organizations. This was amazing because, only a generation before, the Papuans were animistic headhunters. Yet here they were, working shoulder to shoulder with their brothers and sisters from the West, willingly taking on the objectionable jobs that left Western workers reeling.

Christian relief groups do an excellent job of responding to disasters. From antibiotics to food to cash (one boy donated a plastic bucket filled with eighty dollars in change), to time and energy, they are right there to provide whatever they can. And their loving concern is not lost on the suffering. After the 2006 earthquake in Pakistan, a Muslim man who lost everything said, "The Christians are different. They genuinely care by hugging us, praying for us and tending to our needs. They don't just give relief and then leave. They help us for a long time, because they are our neighbors and our friends."

A PLACE OF DEVASTATION

I have been on many rough roads in my travels, but I've never been bounced and tossed around the way I was on the deeply rutted dirt road leading out of Banda Aceh toward an outlying village right in the heart of the tsunami devastation. By the time we arrived, my head ached from repeatedly hitting against the van roof, and I was all in favor of donor support for a vehicle with better shocks.

But the real shock was still to come. Although more than a year had passed since the tsunami had swept over this village, reminders of the devastation were everywhere. Trees still lay where they had crashed to the ground. Tangled piles of debris jammed up here and there. A mass grave—people whispered that it held the bodies of 46,817 people. Almost 80 percent of the area's population had perished in the disaster. Eight out of every ten people.

We crossed a reconstructed bridge on a reconstructed road to a village whose reconstruction we had come to witness. I stopped at the first house and took a picture. So typically Indonesian, intricately decorated, the bright blue house stood on stilts, and in the shade below, hammocks hung from the house supports. "Houses like that used to be common here," said Phil, our guide. "But not since the tsunami. That's the only one still standing. The stilts were supposed to raise the houses high enough off the ground to protect it from floods. But I guess nothing helps when the water comes all the way up to the roof."

On a shaded porch jutting up against the house, an uncommonly tall man with a shock of black hair crouched and silently watched us. He hardly looked forty. Children lounged on the porch around him, and several women too. Also one elderly man. That shade must have felt good; even at mid-morning, the sun was merciless.

"Hello, Santoso!" Phil called to the tall, black-haired man. Santoso flashed a welcoming smile and stood to greet us. He was wearing a black and pink SubZero T-shirt and Levis. Strange. All the women around him were covered from head to toe in typical black Muslim dress.

When he heard we'd come to the village to see how it had progressed since the tsunami, Santoso lamented, "My house was badly damaged, but I won't get a new one. Only those that were totally destroyed get rebuilt. It doesn't seem fair to me."

Waving his hand at the people gathered around him, Santoso added, "Here is what's left of my family." Santoso was away at another village the day the tsunami hit—a trip that may well have saved his life. Yet he's haunted by the thoughts of who all he might have been able to save if only he'd been at home.

"No one," said his father, the elderly man standing behind him. "You could have saved no one. The wave came too fast, and it hit too hard."

Like a bomb exploding, Santoso's father told us, that's how it sounded. Even so, no one thought anything about it. Not even when they saw all the water. They figured it was just the tide coming in especially fast. By the time they saw the wall of water behind that wave . . . well, yes, then they realized something was terribly wrong. But by then it was too late.

"I ran for the bridge, just like everyone else did," Santoso's father said. "I was pulling my wife along with me. But then the water hit us and everything got too confused. All I remember is that I stopped at the bridge and just hung on. I didn't want to cross it. And then I couldn't find my wife. I just stopped worrying about everything and figured whatever happened would happen."

Miraculously, the old man survived. His wife did not. Nor did half of his children and many of his grandchildren. "It isn't right," he said, shaking his head. "Why should an old man still be here and the young ones be gone?" A little girl next to Santoso buried her head in her hands and sobbed.

This one town lost half its population. Many were children. Because the men were out in their fishing boats or preparing for work on the salt flats, it was the women and children, busy with their morning activities, who were in the path of the water. Not one family was left untouched.

In Indonesia, tensions run high between Muslims and Christians.

That's not surprising, for although the country has the world's largest Muslim population, a definite Christian presence exists. Just how large a presence is hard to tell. Many who become Christians stay silent about their faith, since conversion from Islam can mean death.

International organizations had long been banned from the Banda Aceh area of Indonesia's island of Sumatra—especially Christians. This is why Partners International had for years worked in conjunction with an Indonesian partner known by its initials SERASIH. (An organization that includes almost thirty church planters, SERASIH is funded through various churches and organizations both inside and outside Indonesia.) So when the tsunami hit, Partners International was in an especially good position to help out in an area most Christian groups hardly knew existed. Its workers were the first Christians to set foot in some of the outlying totally Muslim villages, in fact.

An enormous job faced them. "Way too many things needed to be done at once," said Phil. "First, of course, the immediate needs of the people had to be met. Then we had to organize projects—so many projects!"

Samaritan's Purse arrived with their expertise in medical intervention and housing. Mission Aviation Fellowship volunteered to fly in relief supplies for the government. World Relief came and began planning other projects.

As the work was getting started, partners of Partners International in Jakarta sent word asking, "How can we help?"

Easy answer: "Send people!" They did so immediately.

"We could see that we and our Western money were of little good if we didn't have people to interface in the village," said Phil. "We needed people who could do the things we foreigners couldn't do. That's where the Indonesians were really able to fill in the gaps. It was a great illustration of the family of God at work."

Certainly many agencies rallied their donors to help relieve the suffering and to get those affected back on their feet as soon as possible. But in following up on the portion of the two million dollars that was donated to just one organization (Partners International) that went to just one area (a village two hours outside Banda Aceh), the following is what I found.

SALT FLATS REPAIRED AND JOBS RESTORED

For three generations, salt farmers have labored in the salt flats on the outskirts of this village, which was banned to foreigners until the floodwaters changed everything. The plot worked by Hamdani, the village leader, had been passed down to him by his father and to his father by his father's father. Ever since Hamdani was a tiny child, he had watched the high tides roll in, wash the dirt with salt water, then roll out again. For as long as he can remember, he has known that the dirt was heavy with salt. Since he could hold a shovel, he helped pile up the dirt and lay it out to dry so that the crusty salt could be taken off. Then, in his family's work hut, a hot wood fire would be built. Huge vats were filled with dirty salt mixed with seawater, and all day long it was left to boil. By evening, the men could shovel pure white salt out of the vats. Now only Hamdani and his brother were left to work the family salt flat.

As I struggled to follow Hamdani's salt demonstration, thick smoke poured from the hut, clogging my throat and choking me. Although the burning in my eyes caused tears to run down my cheeks, Hamdani insisted we go inside the hut and admire the pile of salt. "Taste it," he said. Not so much an invitation as an instruction. Here was a man who took pride in his work.

I couldn't help noticing that he kept squeezing shut his own watering eyes.

Sometimes they ran out of wood, Hamdani told me, and that brought the entire operation to a halt. Also, an overly long rainy season meant big trouble, as did plunging salt prices. But these were known worries—the same ones that had kept his father awake at night, and his grandfather before that. No one ever worried about the barrier dike. In three generations, it had never been damaged. Not until the tsunami. Fortunately Hamdani and the other workers were still at their homes farther up the hill when the wall of water struck. They were still alive, but the dike had been washed away, and the salt flats went with it. A huge part of the village's livelihood was gone.

"Right here was a good place to start rebuilding," Phil told me, "because everything wasn't completely devastated." Together World Relief and Partners International set to work rebuilding sixty-nine processing huts and the entire barrier dike. Within five months, it was completed and all the salt farmers were back at work.

"Is it as good as ever?" I asked Hamdani.

He flashed a huge grin. "Oh, yes!" he said. And as if to prove it, he insisted I brave the blinding smoke and go back into the hut to take one more taste from the pile of white salt.

"It's good," I said, smacking my lips. "It's very good!"

HOMES SWEET HOMES

With most of the village population in temporary barracks, house construction was a top priority. World Relief took the main role in rebuilding homes, while Partners International provided assistance and support. These new houses wouldn't be intricately decorated Indonesian dwellings on stilts like Santoso's house. No, they would be substantial structures of brick and mortar—houses designed to withstand battering waves.

"The more houses we've done, the better we've gotten," said Phil. Mild words to express growing results in spite of a seemingly endless battle just to be able to work. The Aceh Independence Army (GAM)—a separatist group that controls the area—never let up its harassment. Tools and building materials disappeared, even parts of cement mixers!

Several times a day GAM leaders showed up at the building site to demand money—or more. Once they wanted a boat.

"Thankfully we were able to negotiate a way to move forward with the GAM leadership and finally get the house construction back on track," Phil said.

They also had to struggle with a dishonest village chief who plotted to sell off the new houses to people who hadn't even been affected by the tsunami. When GAM discovered the phony deal, they automatically assumed the Christians were in on it. In retaliation, they damaged the houses.

And at every turn, bridges washed out. Or bamboo-reinforced roads needed to be re-reinforced. Or something else happened to prevent access. Because the roads and bridges were so old and damaged, the project grew and grew, both in time and in cost. But in the end, 450 houses were built in the village.

Wonder if it was worth all that? Ask someone who was there. Phil said, "It was so wonderful to see people cleaning up and moving into their new homes!"

A SCHOOL DEDICATED

One really horrible thing was the tsunami's toll on the town's children; over four hundred died. Getting a new school up and running was a major priority, not just to provide the surviving kids with an education, but to give a sense of order to their lives. The temporary building Partners International threw together for them to meet in was just a stopgap. They really needed something permanent.

Once again, World Relief stepped forward with funds for the building. Partners International provided the equipment, such as desks, chairs, cupboards and so forth. Building a school is an enormous undertaking. Yet one year and three months after the tsunami, I had the privilege of witnessing the dedication of the new primary school: six classes, one for each grade, first through sixth; a total of 227 students; and a truly

Excited children starting classes at their new school (by Dan Kline)

amazing thing—half of those students are girls.

"The children have suffered a lot," the school's headmaster told me. "They have a lot of trauma to overcome." (Although he was in another town when the tsunami hit, he hurried home to find his wife and all his children washed away.) "But there is a good side. The children are much more motivated to go to school now."

That puzzled me, so I asked why. Because of the interaction from the outside, he explained. The children and their families had never before seen a woman do anything except work in the house. None of their mothers could do more than sign her name. "When women in the village saw that women from the outside do so many things, they said, 'We want our children to be like that! We want them to have a future too.' That's why you see the girls in school now." For the first time, the village saw that there truly was another way.

At the school dedication, a representative from World Relief stood before us and said, "The children sang a song for us that said, 'I want to be well educated, because I am the leader of tomorrow.' Education is the dream and desire of the children. The teachers and doctors and farmers and business people and governors, and all tomorrow's leaders of this community, are right here with us today."

And it was all made possible because donors' hearts were moved. They dug into their pockets, knowing they were rebuilding a school. But did they realize they were investing in the future of several villages, that they were affecting the direction of people who had never before seen a Christian?

A government leader gave his speech too. He said many things, but what I remember most is this: "We know your love for God because you showed it to our children."

New Boats Mean Hope for Tomorrow

Jaya was a small man whose meticulously trimmed mustache seemed at odds with his calloused hands and rumpled work clothes. He didn't have much to say. His attention was focused on the new boat ready to be ceremoniously launched.

"He's embarrassed," someone whispered. "He hasn't had a real job since the tsunami."

So how had he and his family managed? Jaya shrugged his shoulders at the question and looked at his feet. "Doing anything he can," the other

Jaya, the last fisherman in the village to get his fishing boat replaced (by Kay Strom)

man said. "He has been getting all the bad jobs."

Jaya had been out fishing all Christmas day and night with several friends. Too weary to keep going, he turned his boat around and went home before the others. He pulled his boat up onto the sand, the same as always, then headed up the road to his house for breakfast. Fifteen minutes later, the water hit. Jaya grabbed his two smallest children and ran up a nearby hill. His other children tried to keep up with him, but they couldn't. They were lost. Jaya's friends never made it back to shore.

How could Jaya complain? He had his life. And his wife and two of his children, which was more than most of his neighbors could say. Yet he had lost his livelihood, and every day was a struggle to earn enough to keep his family alive.

If you think that building boats isn't high on the list of needs for disaster funds, take a look at Jaya. About twenty of us—from all around Indonesia, from Canada, from Mexico, from the United States—all worked together to push Jaya's new boat from the builder's work yard down to the beach and out onto the water. Boat number 128. The last of the village's destroyed fishing boats rebuilt and launched.

Each one cost $1,450. Each meant a livelihood for one family. Together those boats were a new beginning for the village.

VILLAGE SHRIMP PONDS

It's interesting, the things people do for a living—and the things they find it difficult to do without. How vulnerable some of the most essential things actually are, such as shrimp ponds.

The ponds are a clever idea. Constructed at the edge of the ocean, their retaining walls keep the tides from flooding them, and gates let the water in and out as desired. Huge shrimp—what we would call prawns—are farmed in these ponds. When mature, the shrimp are scooped out with a net and sold. Depending on the size of the pond and on how well everything goes, a family can earn eight hundred dollars in profit per harvest. And they get three harvests per year.

Besides shrimp, the ponds are stocked with fish—not for selling, but for the family to eat. There are enough fish in a pond so that if the shrimp should get a disease and die, the family won't go hungry. (The ponds also have clams, oysters and crabs, which don't bring in much money but do act as pond filters, keeping it clean.)

Eighty-five families have four-acre shrimp ponds on the outskirts of the village. Or at least they did before the tsunami erased the entire pond infrastructure. With the ponds destroyed, eighty-five families were left without an income—and without food.

The first step in rebuilding the ponds was to reconstruct the retaining walls and the gates. That was Partners International's job. With the purchase of a backhoe, everyone was able to take a turn at plugging the holes in the sea walls. World Relief funded the pond reconstruction, and the United Nations Food and Agricultural Organization provided shrimp to stock the repaired ponds.

The farmers, realizing they had a unique opportunity to improve on their old system, decided not simply to throw the ponds back together. Instead they would allow everyone to buy into the project and construct proper channels.

To teach new and improved shrimp-raising techniques, Partners International and World Relief put together a demonstration pond. Unfortunately, just three weeks before the shrimp harvest, a disease hit the pond and the shrimp had to be harvested while they were still too small to get the best market price. No one lost money, but they didn't make much either. It was a real disappointment.

The second demonstration pond fared much better. Not only was it loaded with huge shrimp, but huge shrimp that were highly resistant to diseases.

KEY BENEFIT: By providing food, housing, medicines and a livelihood to those who are affected by catastrophe, we can demonstrate Christ's love, even in otherwise unreachable areas and to people who would never listen to our words.

KEY CHALLENGE: Internal factions, such as GAM.

CHILDREN'S PROGRAM: *Indonesia*

AND WHEN IT'S TIME TO MOVE ON

Disaster relief is just that, emergency relief in times of catastrophe. Which means it isn't intended to be open-ended. That's not to say disaster relief can't open up areas for ongoing work, but that's a whole different project.

Surely it takes more than a new house and a new boat and a repaired village to make everything right after a calamity. Just ask Santoso or the school headmaster or Jaya or any of the others.

"I can almost tell how many members of a family were lost in the tsunami by looking into a person's eyes," Phil said.

CHILDREN'S PROGRAM

Our partner built a community center to provide activities like crafts, traditional dance, art, sports and reading for the children. These activities have gained support from the community, and children flock to the center after school. Your gift will enable one child to take part in the activities and experience the love of God. . . .**$10/month or $120/year**

Yet the relief efforts for this particular disaster have been completed. In an area where a woman was doing well if she could struggle through the reading of a single sentence, half the primary student body is girls. In an area that had never seen a Christian before the tsunami, people now speak tenderly of the loving help they received from the followers of Jesus. That's not to say there's nothing more for donors to do in the Aceh province of Sumatra. In such a place the door is open and a welcome mat of opportunity is spread out.

THE LIBRARY OPPORTUNITY

Three days each week, as soon as Devi opens the door to the new library, kids crowd in to play games and do crafts and listen to stories. They also reach for the beautiful new books. The kids are hooked.

From the very first day, ten-year-old Sari has always been the first one through the door on library day. She would pick up one picture book after another, point to a picture and ask, "What's that?" then turn the page and ask, "What are they doing here?"

Devi chose a book from the first section—one of the easiest beginner books—and handed it to Sari. "Why don't you read this to me?" she said.

Sari opened the book and looked blankly at the single sentence on the first page. "Can you read at all?" Devi asked gently.

Sari shook her head. "I never held a book in my hand before I came here." Sari was an extremely bright little girl; that was soon obvious, for within six months, she was reading at her grade level. Impossible, you say? Not when willing teachers surround insatiable children in a brand-new library filled with irresistible books.

Children are encouraged to read their books out loud. That way, the staff can pick out any who, like Sari, cannot read. Interestingly the children aren't the least bit intimidated by this. Staff members work individually with those who are struggling—not always an easy task, since the women don't have a background in child development. What they do have is good training from Partners International's network. For instance, short-term teams with education experience come and work with the women, providing them with teaching ideas and fresh approaches.

Many students start school knowing nothing of the Indonesian language; they speak only the local Acehnese dialect. That's a big problem educationally, since all the textbooks are in Indonesian. The staff brings in storybooks to help teach the kids to speak and read Indonesian. At first, many children can only look at the colorful pictures, yet the books are a big hit. The public school teachers and the principal love the children's library program. It makes their job a whole lot easier.

In many ways the library is a lot like school libraries in this country—shelves stocked with a variety of children's books, from the simplest picture books to teen readers, even comic books. Children can check the books out, take them home and keep them for a week. But the library is also different from the ones we know. For one thing, it's much smaller than those even in our small schools. Also, it has a little section for adults—a way to let children know it's all right for adults to read too.

So what's the big deal about a school library, you ask? Well, only about

5 percent of Indonesian schools have any library at all—including universities. What we take for granted is a relatively new concept there. By changing perceptions about reading, the library concept could transform the next generation.

As a matter of fact, the library program has been so successful that a whole new problem has arisen. Sari and some of the other kids have already read every one of the books! "What we would like to do is develop this into a traveling library," said Iwan, an Indonesian businessman from Jakarta who is associated with SERASIH. "People in our Indonesian churches could donate high-quality books their children have outgrown. Then we could take the books from this library to another school and bring an entirely different set of books here. We could have libraries in several places. By keeping the books revolving between them, we could keep all the libraries fresh." Certainly Sari and her friends would approve of the idea.

Some donors are already getting pretty excited about it too. One retired teacher said, "This is my kind of project. Where do I sign up?"

> **KEY BENEFIT: In the aftermath of disasters, a whole variety of new opportunities becomes available.**
>
> **KEY CHALLENGE: It is imperative to proceed with sensitivity, following the lead of the local people, always mindful of what is important and helpful to them.**

CONCLUSION
Making Gift Decisions

Now you have it . . . the rest of a most exciting story.

After seeing the proud owners of cows and goats and pigs; busy medical clinics operating in China; cargo containers arriving in Africa full of life-saving medical equipment; fishermen launching new boats in Indonesia; children with disabilities emerging from the shadows to live productive lives in North Africa and Cambodia; new wheelchairs in Poland; indigenous church planters carrying the good news to the Himalayan Mountains and Nepal and the deserts of Rajasthan; babies born HIV-infected and then enfolded into a loving, nurturing environment; desperate children fed and cared for—after seeing all this and so much more, we begin to grasp the enormity of our potential as donors. We actually see the difference our twenty or two hundred or two thousand dollars makes.

So, are our gifts impacting the world? Absolutely! No question about it.

"The world is a dangerous place, not because of those who do evil, but because of those who look on and do nothing."

ALBERT EINSTEIN

So many groups are now putting out gift catalogs. (Check out the appendix for information on organizations mentioned in this book. Of course, that's only a sampling of what is out there.) And so many others that don't have catalogs make touching appeals online, on television and through the mail. With so many groups working in the world's neediest places and among the most vulnerable people, how do you sort out the good from the not so good? And out of the good, how do you select the best?

Just recently I got an e-mail appeal from a friend that had been forwarded by a coworker who knows someone who's promoting a goat-gifting program in Uganda. The very same week I received a phone call from another friend who was bubbling over with excitement about a sponsor-a-child program operating out of Taiwan. Within days, a letter came in the mail from a group that builds cutting-edge homes for people in disaster areas. All needed money—immediately. All sounded wonderful. All were completely unknown to me. Were these organizations valid and their work worthwhile? I have no idea.

"I'm truly thankful that organizations exist to facilitate this process. It's a blessing to have the opportunity to share our good fortune with others in such a profound way."

JULIE A.

I recently had the pleasure of meeting Pat and Dave, parents of Stephanie and Stacy. I really enjoyed Pat; she's friendly and full of fun. Dave is a man with a heart for the world who, it turns out, causes everyone a real problem at gift-giving time. Stephanie and Stacy are loving daughters who aren't the least bit interested in wasting their limited resources on gag gifts or stuff that will be piled into the closet only to end up for sale at a thrift store. The two girls also happen to be quite clever.

One Christmas, Stephanie and Stacy—who at the time were cash-strapped college students—picked up a World Concern catalog that had come in the mail, and they thumbed through it. When they saw "Banking on Piggies," they knew they had found a Christmas present for their dad. What better gift for a hard-to-shop-for guy who loves to give in a way that will significantly help others than a real live piglet that would grow into a two-hundred-pound mama pig and change the life of a family in Africa? And for just forty dollars? Of course, they couldn't wrap up the pig. So they bought a toy piggy that squealed when it was squeezed, wrapped it in Christmas paper and tied it with a bow, signed it with love and tucked it under the tree. And that's how Dave got the first in what was to become a long line of the best Christmas gifts ever.

"I'm really hard to shop for!"

DAVE L.

Over the years, Stephanie and Stacy have scoured a whole array of donor gift catalogs and websites in search of their just-right dad-gifts. Dave has opened Christmas presents from his daughters to find

- a hunk of goat cheese (a goat for a family in Africa)
- a homemade cardboard fish (fishing supplies to enable a family to start a fishing business)
- cold medicine and a box of bandages (medical supplies to encourage women's health in Egypt)
- a bike helmet (bicycles for pastors in India)
- a scavenger hunt that ended in a closet full of wheelchairs (specially made wheelchairs for Kenya)
- a hymnbook and a Bible (Christian literature for two churches in Cambodia)
- a bottle of water (a well and water filter for a village in Africa)

**One woman went to her friend's baby shower.
Along with a bib and booties, she gave the gift of
prenatal and follow-up care in Senegal.**

Does Dave miss tearing wrapping paper off ties and shirts and books and slippers on Christmas morning? Ha! He eagerly looks forward to his turn when, with all the extended family gathered around, he gets to open his next donation. Of one thing he is certain: his gift will meet a physical need in a way that will open doors to meeting spiritual needs.

One grandma gave her grandchildren an armload of stuffed baby chicks to represent the real chickens she bought and donated in their name.

Many first-time donors tell Partners International that they had been praying for something different and meaningful to give their friends and family as a gift, and then there it was—the catalog in their mailbox.

Judi and Randy A. looked at their newlywed friends, who already had everything, and decided to gift them with the donation of a well for a thirsty North African village. Their friends framed the gift card.

Of course, there are also those who say their mailboxes are stuffed so full of catalogs that they would never notice one more, let alone take time to thumb through it. Or, because everything looked good, they might just put the catalogs aside until they have more time to make a decision—which, of course, is never.

So, back to our question: With such a wide array of choices, how does a wise donor go about making the decisions that will lead to truly effective donations—effective enough to change a life?

"This is exactly what my family, and my three sisters and their families, decided we would do for Christmas this year! None of us needs any more 'stuff.' But we don't know how to start. Where do we look and what do we do?"
BONNIE J.

The following will help you sort through the *ifs, whens* and *buts* of sound giving.

YOUR DONATION IS MOST EFFECTIVE IF . . .

the organization to which you give is financially responsible and scrupulously accountable to its donors.

Scandals, skimming, exorbitant salaries to CEOs, luxurious perks for management and large donors—in our most cynical moments, it's hard not to believe that in this day and age these are simply the new American way. From the government right on down to the church, doesn't everyone take advantage of every possible way to grab hold of more than they should?

Actually, no. Everyone doesn't.

Yet in an area as rife with loopholes as charitable giving, where the most unexpected among us seem able to rationalize outrageous behavior, some people find it impossible to resist the temptation to dip their hands in and grab a little—or a lot—for themselves.

"It's my job to give," one man told me. "It's God's job to make sure it goes to the right place." Really? That doesn't seem to square with Jesus' teachings. In the parable of the talents, for instance, the Master rewarded those who actively and courageously brought about the greatest return on what he had given them (see Matthew 25:14-29). That would indicate that we are required to be good stewards of what God entrusts to us.

Allan, who lives in a tract house and drives an eight-year-old car, is a good example. Even his closest friends would be amazed at the amount he donates to charity. They would be even more amazed at how scrupulously he examines an organization's financial records before he even considers giving to it.

According to a recent survey by the *Chronicle of Philanthropy*, the amount the largest four hundred charities in the United States receives keeps getting bigger and taking in a larger share of the donation pie—

one dollar of every four dollars raised. But despite their high visibility and their well-honed fundraising skills, they are not necessarily the best place for your charitable dollars.

> **"I used to just write a check to one of the well-known umbrella agencies. But I've grown much more wary. Now I check everything out."**
>
> **KATHY C.**

When evaluating a charity, one thing to look for is low operating costs. In many gift donation catalogs, you will find a clear layout of the way funds are used. Other organizations make this information available on their websites. Charity Navigator (www.charitynavigator.com) gives a complete breakdown of a philanthropy, including its CEO's salary. (This doesn't necessarily include his or her complete compensation package, however.) Problem is, Charity Navigator bars some extremely worthy and fiscally responsible charities because it doesn't rate those legally exempt from filing an IRS form 990. (This includes many religious organizations, such as the Salvation Army and Partners International, despite the fact that they voluntarily file the form each year.) Another site to check is Guide Star (www.guidestar.org). Also look for such accountability affiliations as Better Business Bureau and the Evangelical Council for Financial Accountability (ECFA). Or just ask. Contact the charity and say you want to know what percent of the budget covers overhead and how much the CEO takes for salary and other compensation.

Sure, you have a right to know. It's your money!

Because more and more people are demanding proof of financial accountability, more organizations are making this information available, including their audited financial statements. Here is a sampling of what's offered:

• Partners International's Financial Integrity statement offers copies of their annual report and audited financial statements. It also assures donors that the organization is a charter member of the ECFA.

- On its website, World Concern addresses safeguards under the heading of "Frequently Asked Questions," saying that in order to "maintain the highest level of integrity, we are held accountable" by National Charities Information Bureau and ECFA. It also offers access to a summary of its financial records or an audited financial statement.

- World Emergency Relief has links on its website to audited financial statements, annual reports and its IRS 990s, all for the past four years.

> **"What fun! For our combined birthdays, our best friends gave us a thousand dollars to spend in the Partners International gift catalog. We spent the entire month making our choices. You wouldn't believe how far that money went!"**
>
> **KAROL AND ED K.**

"The problem with all of these organizations is that every one of them takes money out for administration and fundraising," several people complained. "I want *all* my donation to go to those in need!" Makes sense. . . . Or does it?

If an organization actually did pass 100 percent of its contributions on to the needy, it would have a tough time staying in business. Without a fundraising budget, how would anyone know it exists? Certainly, watch the percentage that goes to the projects, but don't expect it to be 100 percent. And keep in mind that percentages alone don't tell the whole story. If a CEO's salary is quoted as a percentage of donations received, for instance, take a look at the dollar amount of that person's total package. Some philanthropic organizations bring in a huge amount of money, so a small percentage can still add up to a whopping salary.

Don't completely discount those 100-percent-for-the-projects statements either. Just make certain that you fully understand them. For instance, Direct Relief International promises that 100 percent of all donations given for disaster relief actually go for disaster relief. How is that possible, you ask? Well, first of all, the organization's medical supplies are all donated, so they don't have the cost of goods with which most organizations must reckon. Second, the administrative costs come out of undesignated funds. So where your money goes depends on what you do— or do not—stipulate on your check. While Direct Relief doesn't state what percent of their overall income goes to its actual programs, they do assure donors that for every dollar spent, six people are supported with medicines and supplies worth almost thirty dollars wholesale.

Stephanie and Stacy were not nearly as methodical in their financial analysis as Allan is. Still they quickly noticed a wide price variation from one catalog to another between what seemed to be essentially the same items. Their first purchase—the baby pig—was half the cost of a piglet sent to the same country from another catalog. That certainly made a difference to them.

> **"When I think of making donations, I think in terms of**
> **what all I can get for my money. Like, five pigs and**
> **one well and seven people trained as master trainers.**
> **It's much more fun than thinking in terms of dollars and cents!"**
> **CHRISTINE I.**

Many donors ask, "Will my donation really end up where I intended it to?" Well, often the answer is right in the catalog or at least on the website, but if you want to read it, you may need to keep a magnifying glass close at hand. In some catalogs, the policy is in awfully small print. Several specifically state that contributions will go to the projects selected. When a project is fully funded, however, additional gifts will be used "where they are needed the most." This is understandable, to be sure, and perfectly acceptable to most donors. Most, but not all.

"I want my donation to go for the care and treatment of children with disabilities," said Maria Elena, the mother of Ruben, the boy with Down syndrome. "I know there are many other wonderful causes and lots of needy people. But this is my cause."

So along with her donation, Maria Elena always includes a note that clearly states, "Should this program be fully funded, please return my donation." She explained, "That way, I can send my contribution on to a similar program through a different organization."

And the response? "It's been great. Only once was I informed that the program was already fully funded. But instead of sending my check back, they accepted a little boy into the program who had originally been rejected because of a lack of funds!"

A few organizations state, "Catalog projects are only representative." One included this disclaimer: "contributions are solicited with the understanding" that the organization "has complete control over the use of all funds." We have seen this, for instance, with World Vision's approach to child sponsorship; in most cases, it is the community that benefits from the pooled gifts rather than a single child benefiting from the gifts of her or his specific sponsor.

Again, a representative arrangement is just fine with some donors. For others—such as Kathleen, who donated for building construction and discovered that her gift was used for a staff member's car insurance—it's not at all fine. How about you? The more emphatic your answer, the more vital it is that you carefully read even the smallest of print—or go further and ask direct questions.

**"I've purchased animals from Heifer International
when I've needed a gift for a friend.
It's the difference between giving someone something else they don't
need and giving someone the opportunity of a lifetime."**

DOLORES M.

YOUR DONATION IS MOST EFFECTIVE IF . . .

your goals and expectations agree with those of the organization.

It didn't take Stephanie and Stacy long to determine what they wanted in a gift. Medicine, education and the Bible—that's where their hearts were. But of course the gift wasn't for them. It was important that they chose a project their dad would like, which meant it must be something that would really help people in a significant way.

"We wanted a gift that would help a family care for themselves . . . one that would provide a solution to a need, not just a patch."

STEPHANIE L.

They quickly discovered that more was involved than simply looking at an array of gift possibilities. The organization and what it stood for was also important.

By reading a group's mission statement, you can learn a great deal about its priorities and goals. Here are a few examples:

- Compassion International exists as an "advocate for children, to release them from their spiritual, economic, social and physical poverty and enable them to become responsible and fulfilled Christian adults."

- Direct Relief focuses "on health by providing essential material resources to locally run health programs in poor areas around the world and during times of disaster. DRI is a nonpolitical, nonsectarian organization that provides assistance without regard to race, ethnicity, political or religious affiliation, gender or ability to pay."

- Heifer International states that it is a "humanitarian assistance organization that works to end world hunger and protect the earth."

- Oxfam "delivers development programs and emergency relief services, and campaigns for change in global practices and policies that keep people in poverty."

• World Relief, as the humanitarian arm of the National Association of Evangelicals, "works with the Church to relieve human suffering, poverty and hunger worldwide in the name of Jesus Christ."

Are you especially interested in sponsoring a child or perhaps in fighting world hunger? Do you have a special love for China or for India or for Africa? Are you looking for a Christian-based organization or one that is nonsectarian, or perhaps a group that mixes humanitarian and spiritual endeavors? For many donors, a lot of these conditions don't matter much. But to some, they make a great difference. Wherever your parameters lie, find an organization that fits within them.

> **"We have a Compassion International child in India.**
> **I like it that they make it clear that the money you send**
> **really goes to that specific child."**
>
> **NEIL M.**

QUESTIONS TO ASK

1. What percentage of donations to this organization actually go to its programs?

2. With what oversight group(s) is the organization affiliated?

3. Do you feel strongly about an organization's religious slant or its approach to humanitarian aid in relationship to religious work?

4. Have you read the group's mission statement, including the fine print? How does it match up with your personal goals?

> **"This is an easy way to become involved in missions.**
> **Anyone can save one dollar at a time.**
> **Even a child could do this, or it could be a family project."**
>
> **STACY L.**

Your Donation Is Most Effective When . . .

local people are involved in the decisions and are committed to the project.

After floodwaters washed away several villages in India, a well-meaning organization rebuilt hundreds of houses. The workers used a black building material that seemed especially sturdy. But no one can live in those houses. Turns out they are way too hot. Had locals been consulted, they could have warned that black absorbs the intense Indian sun and turns a house into an oven. But no one asked them, and so today hundreds of rebuilt houses sit empty.

To do an appropriate project in an appropriate way, people from the outside must have good, accurate information. That comes best from people who live locally. This is why Heifer International has the communities in which it works choose the recipients of their animals through a democratic process.

Partnering with the local population is the only real path to healing and hope. Outsiders can provide emergency relief in times of disaster, but they don't go in and fix things for local people. The best any of us can do is empower them to help themselves.

"It is the Christians who have come to wipe away our tears."
TSUNAMI VICTIM TO SAMARITAN'S PURSE AREA DIRECTOR

The best organizations are the ones that look at a project and ask, "Is this the people's vision? Did it come from them?" The best organizations are the ones that work alongside the people they aim to help, and together with them see dreams become reality.

Your Donation Is Most Effective When . . .

the organization builds relationships with people rather than simply handing out gifts.

Every place we went, we spent a great deal of time hanging around talking: eating together in homes in North Africa, drinking tea in India, laughing and visiting in China, in temperatures soaring to 115 degrees in Sudan and while dripping with sweat in Indonesia. I'll have to admit that more than once I sneaked an impatient peek at my watch. But then I would be reminded once again: "These are not just projects; they are relationships. These are real people with real lives"—the man in Senegal who tearfully shared that to keep his job he would have to move his family to a place he didn't know and that didn't know him, the man in Cambodia whose wife chided him because he didn't change into his good clothes when we arrived. Hospitality extended—sometimes at great sacrifice—and gratefully accepted. Food cooked and tea brewed.

Relationships.

"Significance and perspective necessitates being there."
DAVID RAWSON, PARTNERS INTERNATIONAL BOARD MEMBER
AND U.S. AMBASSADOR (RETIRED)

Big philanthropic agencies are able to hand out far more money than small ones. But that doesn't necessarily make them better. Groups committed to relationships establish a presence in an area and stay there for years. They know the people, and they work with them, hand in hand. And they follow up on the projects.

Partnership is far more than just projects and programs. It is the product of time and effort.

"Our Partners International gift this year was a house for someone in India. We figured if we were fixing up our own house, it was a good idea to help with someone else's."
CAROLINE AND PHIL P.

QUESTIONS TO ASK

1. In what ways are local people involved in this project?

2. Is the organization committed to working along with the recipients of the project?

3. What type of follow-up will be done?

YOUR DONATION IS EFFECTIVE, BUT . . .
the unexpected can happen.

Even after the most careful planning, unexpected things happen. Frustrating things. Things that grab a project and yank it around and turn it in a whole different direction.

Cambodia's animal bank has been extremely successful. Cows, pigs, goats, chickens—great ideas all. Actually chickens looked to be the best investment because a poultry company in Thailand contracted to buy all the chickens the bank could raise. A ready-made market—who could ask for more?

But right away difficulties began to crack that perfect donor investment plan. The great Thai company had a few stipulations in small print. All the chicken feed had to be purchased through them, and their cost was far more than "chicken feed." Bank members were paying double what they had expected to pay, and it was really cutting into their profits. The animal bank responded by cutting back on their chicken investments.

Fortunate move. Because soon afterward, when avian flu hit birds in Asia, it was Cambodia that was hit hardest. In a matter of weeks, all the remaining chicks were wiped out. No more Cambodian chicken banks.

Who could have known?

The important element to look for in an organization is honesty, which includes transparency concerning its weaknesses and failures. Several organizations have learned from experience the importance of providing people with basic financial training before giving a loan to set up a small business. More than one reported having financed a goat or a cow only to have it sold "due to family needs." An organization doesn't have to be perfect, but it does have to be accountable.

And it certainly should be open. If you as a donor had invested in the Cambodian chicken bank, you would have a right to know what happened. After all, you just might want to replace the chickens a family lost with a baby pig.

One more thing: If you're looking for spiritual change as a result of your donation, be realistic. Just because you don't see spiritual transformation, it doesn't mean your gift isn't achieving its full purpose. Many of the world's areas most in need of caring donors are also areas where spiritual results come slowly.

> **"I believe in Christianity as I believe that the sun has risen, not only because I see it, but because by it I see everything else."**
>
> **C. S. LEWIS *(THE WEIGHT OF GLORY)***

YOUR DONATION IS EFFECTIVE, BUT . . .
not everything will be exactly your way.

Perhaps you like the idea of an animal bank, but what you want to donate is a lamb, and the organization you favor doesn't have a sheep bank. Shouldn't you be able to request a lamb for a family if that's what you want? Or you want to sponsor a child, but you really have a tender spot for AIDS orphans in Rwanda. Everyone knows there are plenty of AIDS orphans in that country, so why can't you be specific in your request?

Because the programs are already set up with their own guidelines, that's why. And because regardless of how logical your request appears to you, if it doesn't fit in with the existing program parameters, the organization is unlikely to be able to fulfill your requests.

Sometimes you can find a program with another organization that *can* give you exactly what you want (some *do* have sheep banks, you know). Still the more specific your request, the less likely you are to get everything you want. If you want to donate to a women's wheelchair basketball program in Bulgaria, for instance, it may be that such a program doesn't even exist.

There are, of course, appropriate times and good reasons for you to feel uneasy or dissatisfied. If a program is difficult to understand, for instance. Or if you are unable to get the answers to your questions concerning finances and accountability—or you aren't satisfied with the answers you do get. Certainly if the organization has been tainted by scandals. These are good reasons to take your donation elsewhere.

YOUR DONATION IS EFFECTIVE, *BUT* . . .

some projects require ongoing support.

You can buy a cow for a family or fund a well for a village or contribute to disaster relief or choose to donate to a whole assortment of other programs, and your gift will impact the lives of individuals or villages, sometimes in profound ways. Your gift is given. The blessing is extended.

Other gifts, however, require ongoing support. If you agree to sponsor a child in Sudan, for instance, but then you quit after three months, what happens? It's very unlikely that the child will be cut off and left to starve. But it certainly causes difficulties, and it costs the organization more for paperwork to change the child over to a new sponsor. Also the child that new sponsor would have otherwise taken is left waiting. So, before committing to an ongoing project, it's important that you consider the longer view. Are you willing to continue to support that child or that pastor in Bangladesh? If not, perhaps a one-time gift would be best. You just may find that the rewards for giving are so great you can't wait to sign on for the long haul.

QUESTIONS TO ASK

1. If projects have failed to meet expectations, has it been because of carelessness or a lack of planning, or due to unforeseeable circum-

stances? Has the organization demonstrated an ability to learn from its mistakes?

2. If you are dissatisfied with a program, could it be that you are making unrealistic demands? Or is it something about the program itself that is causing you concerns?

3. Should you begin with a one-time gift to a program that doesn't require ongoing responsibility, or are you prepared to make and follow through on a long-term commitment?

Those people you read about in the catalogs, the ones whose pictures you see looking out at you from the full-color pages—you can give them the gift of health, the gift of education, the gift of a livelihood, the gift of hope for the future. And for some, your gift will last for all eternity.

**"For the first time in my life, I go to school without being hungry,
and I am doing well at school.
Before I always begged, lied and stole.
I enjoy the Bible stories, especially the ones about Joseph and Jesus.
I am very happy to be here."**

ALHADJI

THIRTEEN-YEAR-OLD ORPHAN IN TIMBUKTU, MALI,

SUPPORTED BY A PARTNERS INTERNATIONAL DONOR

Epilogue

The book is finished. The stories have been told.

We have seen how, because of thoughtful donations and caring gifts, the daunting realities of today can be transformed into a tomorrow of hope and possibility. But what about that recurring theme of relationships? Is that just for program workers? For employees who live and work in distant countries?

Oh, no. Meaningful relationships are also possible for donors.

Mark and his family did it. When they sponsored Hannah through Partners International, they agreed to send a monthly check for the little girl's support, but their commitment didn't stop there. They also promised to pray for her daily as a family. And when Mark's work takes him to Sudan, which it frequently does, he visits her and takes her gifts from his children. In a very real sense, Hannah has become a part of Mark's family.

My sister Jo Jeanne did it. After she had supported Subhas Sangma for fifteen years, he had become so important to her that she couldn't abide the thought of him struggling from church to church on foot over the rough miles in sweltering heat and through monsoon rains. He wasn't just a responsibility to her—not just a monthly obligation. Oh, no, Subhas Sangma was a friend.

A Little Child Shall Lead
Suzanne Smith and her first-grade class in Southern California did it too.

In the curriculum for her class unit on Africa, Suzanne found a variety of interesting ideas and activities. What she didn't see was a way to teach the children compassion. So when she happened on a newspaper article about a local woman whose organization helped families in the impoverished African country of Niger become self-sufficient by gifting them with animals, she thought, *Perfect! Even a class of first-graders can raise thirty-five dollars to buy a goat.*

So she put the idea to the children. "Shall we do it? It's your decision. We'll vote on everything."

The vote was eighteen to two in favor of the goat. ("I like it," Erik, one of the holdouts, said hesitantly, "but I don't want to give any of my own money.") The plan was for the class to raise the thirty-five dollars during the school year. And, as best they could, to earn the money themselves.

The next morning the money started coming in. "I cleaned my room," the first child reported as she handed over a quarter.

"I swept the walk," said the next. He had thirty-five cents in dimes and nickels.

And so it continued, day after day after day. Whether it was a penny or a dollar bill, everyone clapped and cheered as each contribution clinked into the basket. And each day the children counted out the money and joyfully charted the total.

Three weeks later, when the moms and dads visited the classroom on Back to School night, Suzanne announced that the goat money had already been raised. The children said, "Now let's get a sheep!" Suzanne tried to protest that the project was over, but the kids voted. They named the sheep Daisy.

Every day, more money. And every day the children got better at counting it and adding up totals. Daisy was paid for by the end of October.

The class voted to buy another sheep; Sarah, they called her. For that one week, Suzanne offered to match any money the children earned. But only what they actually worked for, not gifts or found money. So that week the children were especially meticulous in reporting the source of each deposit: "This twenty-five cents is for making my bed, so it can be doubled." "This twenty-five cents Mommy just gave me for the sheep." Twenty-five cents twice is fifty cents, plus one more twenty-five cents equals . . . *seventy-five cents for Sarah!*

Stories were told, reports composed, letters exchanged. Every child in Suzanne's class could locate Niger on the globe. And all were fully aware of what the animals meant to the needy families who received them. Before Thanksgiving, Sarah the Sheep was paid for too.

"Another animal!" the children insisted. But this time the voting wasn't so easy. The donkey (seventy-five dollars) tied with the camel (four hundred). "Not the camel!" one child snorted. "We can't earn *that* much money!" Others agreed with him. So did Suzanne, but it wasn't up to her. She had promised, after all, that the children would decide everything by vote.

They voted to buy *both* animals.

The next day, Jessie brought a quarter and two nickels. "I found them under the couch cushion in our living room," she reported triumphantly. That afternoon everyone rushed home to search under the cushions in their own houses, and the next day children came to school bearing handfuls of change. All except James, that is. He had a dollar bill. "I found my dad's nail clippers under the cushion," he said, "so he gave me this as a reward!"

One boy brought in the five dollars his grandma gave him for his birthday. Not to be outdone, Alex went home and emptied his piggy bank and brought in twenty dollars. When Rachel dropped her dollar in, she said, "My tooth came out last night, and I got this from the tooth fairy!" Everyone started wiggling their teeth and counting their profits.

Still, after all the money the kids had raised for the goat and two sheep, seventy-five for the donkey was a lot of money. Never mind the camel. Then, an idea: Why not sell popcorn at lunchtime? The PTA had

a popcorn machine. Using their new math acuity, the children figured
that if it cost ten cents to produce a bag of popcorn and they sold it for
fifteen cents, each bag sold would mean a nickel in the donkey bank.

"What if we sold the bag for a quarter?" Jessie suggested. "Then we'd
earn fifteen cents!"

"Yeah," said Luke, "and what if we got someone to give the popcorn?
Then we'd make even more!"

With donated popcorn and a raised price, they made 150 bags of
popcorn that first day. In fifteen minutes, it was sold out. The big kids
left standing in line—their mouths watering and the wonderful fragrance of popcorn wafting through the air—booed the little ones who
stood empty-handed and befuddled. (Actually some of the big kids
ended up handing over their money anyway. "Just take it for your donkey," they said.)

They had another class discussion, this time on the laws of supply
and demand. The next day they made four hundred bags of popcorn and
sold it all. The sale, which went on for three days, netted $350. Enough
to pay for the donkey and the camel, which they named Bumpy.

"A goat, two sheep, a donkey and a camel," Suzanne told her class.
"That reminds me of another Christmas." Who would have thought that
a social studies unit could have knocked ajar a public school door that
usually remains so firmly bolted?

In several Christmas-bedecked first-grade homes, another strange
phenomenon was emerging. Moms and dads, peeking at Christmas letters to Santa, found them headed by a common request: *An animal for a
family in Niger.*

Ahhh. The lesson of compassion.

By January, Suzanne's class unit on Africa had long since come to an
end. But try to tell that to the kids. Now they had friends in Niger. And
their goat was there. And Daisy and Sarah and the donkey and Bumpy
the camel. And so Suzanne invited the woman who headed the founda-

tion to come and give the children an update.

The children listened raptly to the presentation, and they watched the video. Then they said, "We want to get something else. What do you need most?"

All the animals they had given were great, the woman from the foundation said. Actually the greatest need of all was for school supplies for the children, but those ran about forty dollars for each child—an awful lot of money and not nearly as much fun as animals. So, whichever animal they voted on would be greatly appreciated.

Animal? No way! "School supplies!" the kids cried. "For everyone in the school!"

"Whoa!" Suzanne said. "Let's set a realistic goal. There are twenty of you in this class. How about school supplies for twenty kids in Niger?"

The money kept coming in. Grandmas and grandpas got wind of the project, and they wanted to help. Moms and dads were not about to be left out. Older kids in the school got excited, and they contributed too. The first-graders put on a benefit musical of Aesop's Fables, which helped a lot. (Tickets cost $2.65 per person—they had voted on the price.) And as the children kept their project going, their math, reading and logic skills soared.

Stunned at the success of what she had thought would be a simple six-week unit on Africa, Suzanne wrote up her project and entered it in a competition for teachers. It was awarded a five-hundred-dollar Impact Grant. That award led to another, also five hundred dollars.

At the end of the school year, Suzanne's class hosted a potluck dinner so that the parents could meet their new friend from the foundation and see her video on the project in Niger. Then Suzanne presented the class's gift—plus the surprise extra thousand dollars from the two awards. Enough for school supplies for thirty-four students! Twenty first-graders went wild.

Before Suzanne found that article in the newspaper, she knew nothing about animal gifting or organizations that did such projects. She had never seen a catalog for gift donations. Fortunately the group onto which she stumbled was sound.

Was the partnership successful? You be the judge: for needy families in Niger, one goat, two sheep, one donkey, one camel and school

Students from Mrs. Smith's first-grade class show the fruits of their labor (by Suzanne Smith)

supplies for thirty-four students—a total of $1,970. And for the twenty children in Suzanne Smith's first-grade class, a lesson in love and compassion of incalculable worth. In the end, every single child had contributed to the project. Yep, even Erik, who wistfully commented on that last day, "I wish we could buy water for all those animals!"

AND SO, A CHARGE

"Children, you show love for others by truly helping them, and not merely by talking about it" (1 John 3:18, Contemporary English Version). Right there is the true test of one's Christianity, isn't it? Love in action. It's natural to respond to great suffering with caring generosity. To want to jump in and do our bit to help. Maybe even get a tax write-off for our trouble. At least to be able to say, "Yes, it is sad, isn't it? Well, I did my part. Why, just the other day, I . . ."

That's natural. What isn't natural is to love and give when no one seems to notice or says thank you. To keep on loving and giving even when the recipient blames you for the problems. To hang in there long after the cameras are turned off and everyone has stopped watching. It isn't natural to build a relationship with someone very different from yourself, whom you are unlikely ever to meet face to face.

"Many of us in the USA have helped victims of hurricanes in our own country," said Jon Lewis, president of Partners International. "And before you know it, another tragedy faces us in another part of the world. However overwhelmed we feel, God has called us to help others in the name of Christ."

And to keep on helping.

It's our responsibility as the ones to whom much has been given. It's also our great honor, for we can give as unto Christ himself.

"We lost everything within seconds," said an Indian fisherman when he received the gift of a new boat. "We never thought there were God's people who care for us. But now we know that in the name of Jesus there is love, care and help."

There is indeed.

APPENDIX

The following is a directory of the organizations referenced in this book.

Christian Aid
www.christian-aid.org
(+44) 020 7620 4444 (U.K. telephone number)

This U.K.-based charity works with people of all faiths and those with no faith at all, helping them to find their own way out of poverty. It works in partnership with supporters at home and with local community groups around the world, helping to build a global movement for change.

Compassion International
www.compassion.com
1-800-336-7676

Compassion International is a Christian child advocacy ministry that releases children from spiritual, economic, social and physical poverty and enables them to become responsible, fulfilled Christian adults.

CrossLink International
www.crosslinkinternational.net
1-703-534-5465
1-901-323-8477

CrossLink supplies medical mission teams, humanitarian aid organizations, free clinics and hospitals with medicines and supplies in order to reduce suffering among the world's most needy.

Direct Relief International
www.directrelief.org
1-805-964-4767

Nonsectarian, nongovernmental and apolitical, Direct Relief International provides its services without discrimination. Its mission is to improve the health of people living in developing countries and victims of disasters by strengthening the indigenous health efforts of its international partners, providing them with essential medicines, supplies and equipment.

Heifer International
www.heifer.org
1-800-422-0474

Heifer International works with communities to end hunger and poverty and to care for the earth. Its strategy is to have people share their animals' offspring with others—along with their knowledge, resources and skills—and so to expand a network of hope, dignity and self-reliance that reaches around the globe.

International Aid
www.internationalaid.org
1-800-968-7490

Serving as a network of mission hospitals, clinics, orphanages and churches across the globe, International Aid uses its missionary assistance, medical support, compassion ministries, and relief and development services to reach out to those in need, regardless of nationality, ethnicity or creed.

Joni and Friends International Disability Center
See Wheels for the World.

MAP International
www.map.org
1-800-225-8550

With a mission to advance the total health of people in the world's poorest communities, MAP works in community health development, disease prevention and eradication, and global health advocacy. It provides high-quality, FDA-approved medicines and supplies to more than 115 nations.

Oxfam UK
www.oxfam.com
www.oxfamunwrapped.com (catalog)
1-800-776-9326 (U.S. telephone number)

An international confederation of twelve organizations working together with over three thousand partners in more than one hundred countries, Oxfam seeks to find lasting solutions to poverty, suffering and injustice. Its goal is to achieve greater impact through collective efforts. A major thrust of this organization is to increase worldwide public understanding that economic and social justice are crucial to sustainable development.

Partners International
www.partnersintl.org
www.harvestofhope.org (catalog)
1-888-887-2786

Partners International is a global ministry that works to create and grow communities of Christian witness in partnership with God's people in the least Christian regions of the world. It identifies strategic indigenous ministries already begun, then provides an array of resources that strengthens them and helps them develop.

Partners International Canada
www.partnersinternational.ca
1-800-883-7697

This organization brings Canadians into partnership with indigenous Christian ministries for the purpose of advancing God's kingdom. They feed children, help women start small businesses, provide clean water and establish churches that will care for entire villages.

Samaritan's Purse
www.samaritanspurse.org
1-800-353-5957

Reaching hurting people around the world with food, medicine and other help in the name of Jesus Christ is the goal of Samaritan's Purse. Its emergency relief programs provide desperately needed assistance to victims of natural disaster, war, disease and famine. It also works in community development and vocational programs, providing educational and practical help for vulnerable children and assisting with medical projects.

Sisters In Service
www.SistersInService.org
1-770-783-1665

A nonprofit organization dedicated to working with and on behalf of women and children, SIS exists to mobilize and equip advocates to extend God's love to this largely neglected segment of the population through local partnerships in the least-reached places in the world.

Wheels for the World
www.joniandfriends.org
1-818-575-1775

Wheels for the World, an evangelism program of the Joni and Friends International Disability Center, collects thousands of used but serviceable wheelchairs, which are restored by prison inmates and then distributed around the world by teams of specialists. This organization also distributes Bibles and Christian literature and holds disability training for ministry workers in churches.

World Concern
www.worldconcern.org
1-800-755-5022
1-206-546-7201

For nearly fifty years, this Christian humanitarian organization has been providing emergency relief and community development to families. Today they operate in more than thirty countries located in some of the world's most neglected areas.

World Relief
www.worldrelief.org
1-443-451-1900

Founded in 1944 as the humanitarian arm of the National Association of Evangelicals, World Relief works with, for and from the church to relieve human suffering, poverty and hunger worldwide in the name of Jesus Christ.

World Vision
www.worldvision.org
www.worldvisiongifts.org (catalog)
1-888-511-6511

By tackling the causes of poverty, this Christian relief and development organization is dedicated to helping children and their communities worldwide reach their full potential. Motivated by faith in Jesus and as a demonstration of God's unconditional love for all people, it serves the poor, regardless of religion, race, ethnicity or gender.

ABOUT PARTNERS INTERNATIONAL
Real Hope. Real Change. Real Partnership.

Every autumn we at Partners International release our *Harvest of Hope* gift catalog, giving people an opportunity to bring real hope and real change to the least Christian regions of the world. As you have read in this book, these things really happen. People do receive hope, and lives are changed.

We strive to imitate the ministry that Jesus modeled: reaching out in compassion to the "harassed and helpless" to alleviate human suffering in word and deed. Providing compassionate assistance demonstrates God's love and the transforming power of the gospel and its kingdom values.

Since 1943, Partners International has operated from the belief that across the globe local Christians with strategic and innovative ideas are bringing the gospel to their neighbors. We work to identify and partner with indigenous leaders of vision and integrity to advance God's kingdom. The stories in this book testify to the tremendous fruit of those partnerships, as do these results from 2006:

- 72,490 new Christian believers
- 11,300 leaders trained in more effective ministry
- 1,380 churches planted
- 336,720 people helped through relief and development

Many of our supporters use the *Harvest of Hope* gift catalog to make a personal gift. Others share the catalog with family, friends and colleagues. Many use it to give gifts to—or in honor of—others during Christmas, on birthdays, Mother's Day, anniversaries and other occasions.

If you want to participate in this life-changing program, please call us toll-free at (888) 887-2786 or go to www.harvestofhope.org.

PARTNERS INTERNATIONAL
1117 E. Westview Ct., Spokane, WA 99218
(509) 343-4000
www.partnersintl.org
(800) 966-5515

Partners International is a global ministry that works to create and grow communities of Christian witness in partnership with God's people in the least Christian regions of the world.